Seven Ways
to
Lighten Your Life
before you
Kick the Bucket

First published in 2015 by Redshank Books

ISBN 978-0-9930002-8-7

Cover by George Simons and Walt Hopkins

Printed by Lightning Source

Redshank Books
Brunel House
Volunteer Way
Faringdon
Oxfordshire
SN7 7YR

Tel: +44 (0)845 873 3837

Redshank Books is an imprint of Libri Publishing

www.libripublishing.co.uk

Dedicated to the ones we love— and especially to

Our parents:

Genevieve and George

Harriet and Dean

And our lifetime friends:

The Stargazers

George's men's group.
Left to right:

Bill Mahkovitz, Don Pomeroy,
George Simons, Ken Hockenberry,
Steve Schulz, Gene Milburn
(Ari Marcus and Jonathan Levy
not in photo).

The Fine Nine

Walt's support team.
Clockwise from top:

Rosie Hopkins, Den Winterburn,
Joep de Jong, Sushma Sharma,
Jenny Saunders Gilders,
Johnny King, George Simons,
Marianne Erdelyi, Jasenka Gosjic

ACKNOWLEDGEMENTS

The leather bucket on the cover was aboard a ship called the *Mary Rose* when it sank off Portsmouth in 1545. The bucket was found when the *Mary Rose* was raised from the seabed in 1982. The photo is © Mary Rose Trust. See http://www.maryrose.org for more about the *Mary Rose*.

We thank Giovanni Sartori of the London City Hotel, who encouraged us to sit in his café for hours as we did our first work on this book. Jim Dustin created the frog and crocodile avatars. He is at *Jim Dustin, Design* on LinkedIn. With gratitude to everyone we have learned with, we thank some specific people who inspired us as we created this book.

Walt is grateful to	George is grateful to
Frank Barrett	Diane Asitimbay
Dick Beyer	Dave Beckman
David Berlew	Joellen Burns
Dick Bolles	Steve Crawford
Roy Fairfield	Elmer Dixon
Corinne Fleischer	Grant Douglas
Dina Glouberman	Rose Gordy
James Graham	Wieke Gur
Jim Hagerty	Ward Kaiser
Roger Harrison	Ken Nickels
Peter Honey	Cynthia & Armando Milani
Giles Hopkins	Asparouh Nikolov
Nikos Kazantzakis	Julie O'Mara
Jim Lord	Emese Pozdena
Runa Mackay	Cathy Puccinelli
Sonia Nevis	Alan Richter
Alan Raleigh	Earl Rohleder
Herb Shepard	Paul Schafer
David Sparks	Patrick Schmidt
Ilya Sloutsky	Tom Shubert
Stephanie Winston	Martin Sims
Benjamin Zander	Marietta Starrie
Class of '66 Reunion Team	Nico Swaan
YES Kinross Team	Terry Taucer Samson
My family in the US	Paul Westlake
My family in Scotland	Paul Wysocki
and the Fine Nine	The Stargazers Men's Group

TABLE OF CONTENTS

BEFORE THE BUCKET

Introduction:

Who we are, how the book works, and why we wrote it.

IN THE BUCKET

Seven ways to lighten and enlighten your life:

1: Chucket—Dump the stuff you don't need or want.

2: Shucket—Keep what's important but distill it.

3: Ducket—Dodge demands that others throw at you.

4: Fucket—Trash what no longer works for you.

5: Plucket—Grasp the sweets that life still offers.

6: Trucket—Walk your talk and follow your dreams.

7: Tucket—Tell yourself what's working in your life.

BEYOND THE BUCKET

Epilogue:

Beyond the …ucket Lists. Stay in touch.

Notes:

Attributions, Contributions, and Sources

How old would you be if you didn't know how old you are?

Satchel Paige[1]

A man needs a little madness—or else
he never dares cut the rope and be free.

Nikos Kazantzakis[2]

The Method in our Madness— and the Madness in our Method

To give you an idea of the method in our madness, we will first tell you how this book works—and why we wrote it.

And then, to give you a sense of the madness in our method, we will tell you about ourselves—and more about why we wrote this book.

How this book works

If you kick a bucket, it hurts less when the bucket is empty. So, before you kick **the** bucket, be sure that you have drained its fullness and that the bucket is as empty as you can make it. In other words, before you die, live your life to the full.

This book is our reaction to the idea of making a list of things to do before you kick the bucket.[3] A bucket list[4] is a list of *things to do* before you die. Our …ucket lists are *ways to live* before you die.

Our own experience is that we work on all seven ways simultaneously. But you can't write a book that way, so we start with ways to *clear* your life and end with ways to *enjoy* your life. The first four ways help you dump the useless stuff out of the bucket, while the other three ways help you relish what's left in the bucket. Or, as Yoda[5] might have put it:

Before the bucket you kick
Empty out what's crappy
And from what's left then pick
The things that make you happy

Although we like all kinds of poetry, that particular poem[6] is close to the doggerel end of the spectrum. Still, it could be verse. Because we like rhymes—and because the original idea for these lists came from one particular rhyme—each of our seven ways does rhyme with bucket.

Just remember, these Seven Ways are not prescriptions for pills to take; they are descriptions of thrills to make—ways to feel and to be truly alive.

We have set up this book in seven chapters. Instead of tasks to do, each chapter offers ways to live. We tell you stories from our own lives and we encourage you to think of stories from your own life. We show you lists of ways we live our lives and we encourage you to consider how you live your life. We even give you some questions for you to think about and talk about with others.

Here are brief summaries of the Seven Ways that we have developed. If some ways interest you more than others, just start reading those chapters. It's your book and it's your life.

Seven Ways
- to empty your life and lighten your life
- to fill your life and enlighten your life

1. Chucket: Dump things you no longer need in your life.

Look at all the stuff that the years have allowed you to collect on shelves, in cupboards or closets, in the basement or the garage, or even in offsite storage. We figure that since we're not going to keep all this stuff for eternity, it might be a good idea to unclutter our lives and start chucking stuff now. Let's face it, Final Destination Airlines, even more than EasyJet, insists that, "You can't take it with you." Final Destination doesn't even allow hand luggage, no matter how much you're willing to pay. So if you can't take it with you, maybe now is a good time to Chucket.

2. Shucket: Shuck the wrappings and keep the gift.

 Reluctant to chuck it? Maybe there is something you want to keep, but it is encrusted or surrounded with stuff that seems shabby or useless. Just as you can shuck the husk from an ear of corn to get at the corn itself, you can shuck other things in your life. Whatever it is, get to the heart of the matter, peel away and strip off the nonessentials, so you can know what is left and use it to the full. When you Chucket, you throw out the whole thing; when you Shucket, you choose what you really want to keep in the bucket of life—and you distill those things to their essence with careful shucking.

3. Ducket: Dodge demands that don't fit your values.

 When someone offers you another thing to have or another thing to do, then you can accept it or you can duck it. People may feel that you have nothing but time on your hands, so they offer you something to do to keep you from being bored. This task can even come with a wonderful title, designed to flatter you into doing something that doesn't fit your values or just isn't how you want to spend your time. Flattery can get you into trouble. If it isn't for you, Ducket!

4. Fucket: Dump what you're fed up doing or being.

 To clean up your life, sometimes you just need to say, "Fuck it." Identify what you have been doing out of habit, compulsion, or just being too nice. Maybe you're tired of doing something, having something, or being something that is no longer working for you. Maybe you're just doing too many things and you want some time for yourself. Instead of a bucket list of things to do, this is a Fucket List of things **not** to do. If it's causing you—and perhaps others—pain or aggravation or if it's squandering your time or energy, then it's time to say, "Stop already!" That's the Fucket moment. That's when you have finally Stucket in the Fucket Bucket.

5. Plucket: Reach for what you still want to do and be.

Delight in the stuff that you enjoy. Pluck it! The tree of life is offering you possibilities, like ripe fruit hanging on its branches, that you have not paid attention to, or said "maybe later" to, or simply said "no" to. It's there for the taking, so Plucket! The fruit may be small or large. It may be a momentary delight or it may be the beginning of a new way of living your life. Replenish your bucket for the journey toward your most important visions and dreams.

6. Trucket: Keep on truckin' by doing what you love.

If you're still alive, you haven't completed the purpose of your existence, so keep on truckin'[7] just as the 1960's cartoon encouraged us to do. We've updated that to Trucket! Do what you do well. Do what you love with people you love. Enrich others—and yourself—with your skills, your knowledge, your vision, your commitment. Use the wisdom you have been developing and the insights you have gained to improve your relationships, your community, your society.

7. Tucket: Appreciate what you have gained—and given.

"Tucket" is an elderly English word for a trumpet fanfare, often used in Elizabethan plays, and often accompanied by the tuck (or beating) of a drum. Even if you expect to hear a tucket after you kick the bucket as you enter whatever paradise or peace your faith or philosophy promises you, don't wait! Give yourself a drum roll and a trumpet fanfare now! Appreciate the thanks of others for what you have made happen. Appreciate the needs you have met in yourself and in your world. Recall the moments of goodness, kindness, persistence, and success. Celebrate yourself with a Tucket.

Why we wrote this book

Like so many good things in life, this book resulted from a conversation between two dear friends. We were having dinner on the occasion of George's 75th birthday and Walt's 69th birthday. Neither of us is very decrepit—actually we've been feeling great—but we're getting up there. So, given the occasion, it was not surprising that we talked about ageing and about dying—two intimate subjects that can scare the hell out of a lot of people and often create more worries than camaraderie.

We both love playing with words. We both write a daily poem, usually a haiku, to get things rolling in the morning—always, of course, with gratitude to Basho, the Japanese master of haiku.[8]

If you want to know more about Basho—or if you want to know the source of the ideas and quotations that we have sprinkled through this book, just go to the Notes section at the back.

We think puns are funny and that some of the best fun is punny. We often exchange the best word plays (or the worst ones) that come our way or that we create.

We not only play with words—we make them up. Walt, for example, invented a word (with help from George to confirm that the Greek was accurate) to describe one of his favorite pastimes. *Arithmodigmaphilia* (a love of number patterns)[9] is a passion for noticing combinations of numbers in dates—especially ones that work on both sides of the Atlantic so that it doesn't matter which way people write the date: with the month first or with the day first. For instance, 11-11-11 means both 11 November 2011 and November 11, 2011.

However, when we hit 2013, the month combinations ran out for the next century or so, leaving Walt in the lurch for a bit longer than he can probably manage to wait. But he has now named another old habit as *philoheptomathea* (a love of seven learnings), which you will notice throughout this book. So, with George's knowledge of classical Greek, we continue to create meaningful trivia!

REFLECTIONS
Our intention in writing this book is to share our learnings rather than our teachings. We hope to inspire you to develop your own learnings. So we will share our own stories and our own ideas—and remind you occasionally to reflect on what you are thinking to yourself as you read.

Inevitably, in our geriatric birthday conversation, the topic of a "bucket *Here's the first Reflection question: What have you created or experienced as the result of a close friendship?*

list" surfaced, inspired by Justin Zackham's great script[10] for Rob Reiner's fun film with two of our favorite cinema stars, Jack Nicholson and Morgan Freeman. On that particular evening, we were both at a bit of a loss to identify our own items for such a list. This did not bode well, and perhaps hinted at depression rather than a lack of imagination, which has hardly ever been the case between the two of us.

But, on reflection, it seemed rather that both of us have lived somewhat full, good, and satisfying lives. George recalls once having a girlfriend who, though she could buy and sell him ten times over in terms of financial prowess, was incessantly on the prowl for every next *greenback, balle, rijksdaalder,* or *quid* (relationships were more complicated before the euro). George shared his misery about her miserly misanthropy with Walt, complaining, "She's rich. What does she need more for?"

To which Walt, not commiserating, responded, "No, no, she's not rich; *you* are." George goes, "Whaddya mean?" Walt, echoing the

Stoic philosopher Seneca,[11] goes, "Well, you're satisfied with whatever you have. That makes you rich. She is not satisfied with all that she has, and that makes her needy." We sense that our own neediness as we get older may be about a lack of meaning or at least a fear of a limited, fragile framework for life. We intend this book to be anecdotally antidotal.

> REFLECTION
> *If you sometimes feel needy, how do you manage that? What real needs are unmet?*

So what did we do when we got stuck on the bucket list? When stuck, play with the words! And we did. In order to make space in our minds to imagine a good bucket list, we began listing ways to enjoy the everyday good life as it is lived "over the hump" and create a quality lifestyle for older folks like us. In discussion with each other and some friends, we came up with the seven ways that you have just read above. Most importantly, we have been trying them out in our lives and sharing them with others—and *they work!*

The bucket list itself, of course, points at all *the things we want to do and need to do* before kicking the bucket and diving into the tunnel of light. When we talk of bucket lists, it is usually things we want to see or places we want to go, things we want to make, or books we want to read. Beyond that are hugs we want to give and get, or people we want to sort things out with before we go.

When George mentioned to his friend and colleague Gordon Clay that the two of us were writing this book, Gordon remarked, "I really don't need a bucket list. I'm doing exactly what I want and enjoying it enormously." We should all be so lucky! Founder and prime mover of the National Men's Resource Center,[12] Gordon has for many years dedicated his waking moments to enhancing the quality of men's lives. Even if you, like Gordon, are doing what pleasures you in most every sense of the word, you may still do it better, longer, and more satisfyingly with some of the approaches we suggest here.

Our plan is to discuss the how, why, and where of adopting these seven ways by illustrating them with our own experiences. As we suspected, although we had trouble coming up with bucket lists of our own when we first started, we learned that addressing some of these other tasks made mental and chronological space available for what we were really after, helping us identify what we need to complete our lives, or at least make them fuller. So, paradoxically, the bucket list takes shape as we go along, not because it is less important but because we now know more clearly what we want on the list.

We did warn you about our delight in puns. So, although this book began as our reaction to bucket lists, we intend it to be more than a pail imitation. In fact, we intend to go beyond the pail, and (with apologies to Procul Harum) we are aiming for a wider shape of pail.[13]

Significantly, George's first great backpacking excursion was wandering the island of Serendib solo. This led him from the Buddha's tooth to the Buddha's footprint, past Sigiriya's mountain maidens, as well as via jungle paths with the biggest damn spiders he'd ever seen, not to mention the offer of an elder daughter as wife from a family that invited him to dinner. He was experiencing serendipity on the very island (Serendib—now known as Sri Lanka) that gave the name serendipity[14] to that wonderful phenomenon of discovering things by chance.

So, we don't want you to look at our suggested approaches as another discipline, but as a kind of invitation to poke about the ancient monuments and everyday markets of your own Serendib, to see what's there, so that you can, as George's father used to say, "Do what pleasures you." So start where you will and delight in serendipity.

Try the routes we have marked out—but remember, the map is not the territory. As Yogi Berra said, "When you come to a fork in the road, take it."[15] Like many of Yogi Berra's great lines, there is hidden wisdom. When you come to a fork in the road, you could just stop there—frozen with indecision. Yogi is saying that you need to keep on truckin' by deciding to go somewhere. When you come to a choice, then pluck it or duck it, or whatever. Pluck what works for you, and duck, chuck, or fuck the rest.

Our hope is that you will find this book both enlightening and entertaining, but most of all stimulating, as you take a good look at what remains on your plate, as well as what choices the menu offers as your just desserts, along with the leisure time for a good digestive.

> *REFLECTION*
> *Serendipity. What things have you discovered by accident, by wandering about, or by just being curious? How have they enriched your life or changed how you live?*

Though some of our best friends are women, we are writing as guys for guys. In a classic joke, a guy on a California beach finds and rubs a lamp that turns out to have a jinni in it. The jinni offers a single wish, so the guy, who hates flying, asks the jinni to build him a road to Hawaii. The jinni complains, "Hey, that's a lot of work—isn't there something else you'd rather have?" The guy, echoing Siggy Freud,[16] asks, "Tell me what women want." The jinni goes silent for a moment, and then meekly asks, "Two lanes or four?"

On the other hand, if you are a woman who is equally puzzled about what it is that men want, maybe you can find a few answers in this book!

Although we began writing this as two older guys writing for other older guys, we are reasonably certain that people who aren't guys and who aren't older will still want to read at least some of this just to keep an eye on us—to find out what the geezers are up to now.

So, welcome to our ...ucket musings. May they serve you well. Let us know what you learn. We have created an online site[17] at https://www.facebook.com/bucketbookviews for your reactions and for further sharing from you and from all of us in a place (with gratitude to Rumi)[18] beyond judgment where we can all stretch out in the cybergrass to tell stories, ask each other questions, and perhaps write a poem or two. See you there!

Who we are and how that led to this book

Before going forward, you might want to know more about who we are and why we are doing what we do. Throughout the book you will find bits that are directly from our own experience. Sometimes we write as both of us—and then we use the pronoun "we" to indicate that.

Other times we write as individuals—and then we use the pronoun  "I" to indicate that. So you know who the "I" is, we put a small favorite beastie at the beginning of each "I" section. George's wee beastie is the little crocodile— reminiscent of Schnappi in a German children's song. Walt is a great fan of both Jim Henson and Kermit (Jim Henson's Muppet creation of Sesame Street fame)[19] so naturally his wee beastie is a frog.

Yup, kid stuff, but note, we are not in our second childhood; rather, we are still in our first—*puer aeternus* in what we hope is the best  sense of those words: ever playful. And yup, adult stuff: these avatars are serious as well as playful. They are our totem animals with all sorts of meaning for us. Just as an example, both avatars are amphibious—which fits with how both of us move among different cultures in our lives and in our work.

"Schnappi" & "Frog" in real life

As a "we" with two "I's" we will tell you stories from our shared experience and our individual experience. We will also tell you stories that others have shared with us. And we will offer you some ways to go forward from those stories. So let's begin.

Of Works and Days—listening to ourselves

"Potter is ill-disposed to potter, and carpenter to carpenter, and the beggar is envious of the beggar, the singer of the singer."

In the words above, the classic poet Hesiod noted that dissatisfaction about who we are and what we do can lead to envy 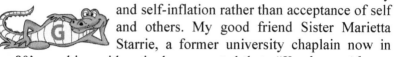 and self-inflation rather than acceptance of self and others. My good friend Sister Marietta Starrie, a former university chaplain now in her 80's working with retired nuns, noted that, *"You hear with new ears once you put on a few years!"* This goes for how you listen to yourself, your past, and everyday conversations with others. We are always talking to ourselves, so why not listen in? What are we saying? In what tone of voice? On trial for his life, Socrates is supposed to have said, "The unexamined life is not worth living." We might add that, "The unlived life is not worth examining."

> *REFLECTION*
> *What is your inner voice saying to you as you read this page? Words? Images? Feelings?*

Listening to yourself, no matter how late in life, will help you drain your life's bucketful for as much joy and satisfaction as you can manage. We are writing this book because we are trying to do this for ourselves—and we invite you to join us. Without disparaging the classical notebook and pen, there are many ways of journal-keeping today, depending on whether you want an audience or not, and, if so, who it should be. You may already enjoy a blog, a Facebook account, etc. Choose what pleases you and serves you best.

Owning up to ourselves

A famous novelist began his autobiography by saying that he was now ready to write his story because he had come to peace with himself about his past, not just the things he was proud of, but even those he was ashamed of. Both could now be woven into the whole fabric of self-understanding and self-acceptance. Some of us experienced racial or ethnic or class discrimination for who we were, or were rejected by someone we loved or respected. There is stored-up hurt to deal with. Owning up to such key items in our bucket helps us lighten the load, access the rest, and increase our joy at each step along the way.

A big part of my life's work has been to reflect and help others to reflection, self-knowledge, acceptance, and change. I have done this through showing people how to use a personal journal[20] in workshops, articles, and books for over forty years and providing my clients with gestalt-based coaching.

Most recently I have been fostering reflection in which I explore for myself and show others how to identify and understand the flow of cultural discourse that they carry within them and the narratives they use to shape their identity in a multicultural world. Echoing old Will Shakespeare, I call the seminar, "What's in a name?" and explore how our identity discourse may start with what we are called at birth and as life goes on.

Some of us are named after our relatives or given religiously revered names like Mohammed or David. Others are called after historical or mythological characters like Alexander, or Attila, or Tristan. Some get honorifics like the two nation builders Mustafa Kemal who was called Ataturk (Father of the Turks) or Nelson Mandela called Tata (also Father in his native language).

Some names make us proud, others make us cringe or even run from them. My immigrant family on my father's side had a Croatian name at a time when the Western Reserve[21] in Northern Ohio was less than welcoming to immigrants.

With my Dad tiring of being called "Simonovich the sonofabitch," I was spared the ignominy by a name change to "Simons." My parents even trimmed my newspaper birth announcement, thinking it might help their posterity to prosperity. It took me a long time to own up to this. Reflection leads to honesty and peace but only if we choose to be ourselves and accept our history to the full.

We all have things that we are proud of and rightfully should be (see the chapter on Tucket) and we also have things that we may be less proud of in our own histories, whether our own actual behaviors, or judgments that others have laid upon us, or which we fear they will lay upon us should they know them about us. Encouraging you to reflect is not an invitation to

*   *   *

Introducing Mr. and Mrs. George Simon and the junior member of the family. George promised to furnish us with a picture when the youngster was born.

advertise your pain, confess peccadilloes or reveal your dirty little secrets, but simply to suggest that things you may not want to look at may deserve a second look in order to integrate them into who you are today and be at peace with them.

Writing these pages, and sharing examples from our own lives has made the two of us realize the importance of coming to grips with discomforts about ourselves, and setting them to rest, paradoxically and above all, enabling us to give thanks all along the way. "Pain is inevitable. Suffering is optional."[22]

REFLECTION
Think for a moment about where the proud and painful places are in your memory.

Setting things right
Apologies and forgiveness, and, where necessary, restitution,

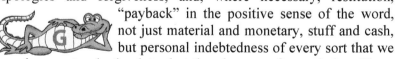

"payback" in the positive sense of the word, not just material and monetary, stuff and cash, but personal indebtedness of every sort that we may have not only the duty, but the pleasure of completing. These are items to consider in making your Bucket List.

Of course there is the practical matter of winding up your affairs: writing a will, and perhaps setting up a succession plan, if you have a business or a project that requires it.[23] If you want your spirit to float free both now and later, that means not encumbering others with your loose ends. Given the uncertainties of life, this is good advice for any adult—and our advancing years make it ever more important.

> *For a list of tasks ranging from setting up a living will and creating a power of attorney to leaving clues about your online passwords and a record of where things are for whoever has to clean up after you, see our suggestions in the Notes section (at Note 23) at the end of the book. We also refer you to other sources of help and information.*

When you have created the legal version of your last will and testament, perhaps—given the reflection involved—you will begin thinking about what your last statements will be about your life. What will you will yourself to do? What will you attest to as important for you and for others in this world?

> *REFLECTION*
> *What might you need to do to get ready for the final trip and make your departure easier for others?*

A goal is a dream taken seriously

As the *Book of Joel* says, "Your old men shall dream dreams, and your young men shall see visions."[24] I am encouraged by Joel's wisdom. Young men do see visions, but old men can still dream dreams—serious dreams.

Many years ago, when I began working with people who were designing their careers and their lives, I developed a statement that is probably the best thing I've ever said: "A goal is a dream taken seriously."[25] I combine those words with the image of a castle on a rock. The image backs up the words. It's important to dream—like a castle that rises starward. And it's important to take that dream seriously—like a castle that you build on solid rock.

In one sense, this book on seven ways to lighten your life is a version of a process I learned from John Crystal and Dick Bolles.[26] If I'm deciding where I want to live or what I want to do, there is a simple three-step approach: first, make a list of what I don't like about a group of factors (such as places to live or things to do); second, convert each of those negative factors into a  factor that is positive for me; and then third, set priorities on the factors—to see which factors are most important to me.

I call this the BSW process: *Bitch* about things you don't like; *Switch* them to things you do like; then choose *Which* things are most important. If you don't think men can bitch,[27] then we could have a conversation about that at our **Bucket Book Views** site at https://www.facebook.com/bucketbookviews or you could choose to call the process ISW for Itch Switch Which, or DSW for Ditch Switch Which.

When I work with people—as individuals, small teams, or groups of a hundred or more—I often use that process of removing the negative to focus on the positive. And in this book we are encouraging you to use a similar process: clear your life's bucket now so as to have space to fill it up for the next part of your life.

When you have begun to pluck those positive things for the next stage of your life, you need to keep shucking them as well so that you focus clearly on what you most want to have and do and be. Those few things are your Serious Dreams. When I worked with a Russian client of mine recently, the result of our two days together was one full-scale Serious Dream for the next few years—and three specific Serious Dreams for this year.

Whether you call it a Bucket List or a Serious Dream, we are intent on the future. Since a Bucket List is about what you want to do before you kick the bucket, you run the risk of putting things off because you are planning for the long run.

John Maynard Keynes famously said that the difficulty with the long run is that in the long run we are all dead. But after he had gained even more wisdom with age, Keynes quoted himself and then offered the opposite point of view to encourage wise choices—*because in the short run we are still alive.*[28]

Each of the …ucket ways in this book is a way of clearing the ground and making choices so that you can focus on your own Serious Dream—sooner rather than later!

Now it's your turn. Throughout this book, as you have already seen, we will give you questions to discuss with others and to think about on your own—perhaps using a journal as George has already suggested.

As you apply what you are learning, you will not be alone. Both of us are continuing to apply to ourselves what we are suggesting to you. I'm still writing in my journal 57 years after I started it and I'm still talking with my friends—some of whom I've been talking with for 40 or even 60 years. You may want to experience this book on your own or you may want to discuss it with friends. You may want to blog about it with us or with others. Up to you. Choose your own way of learning as you go.

Roots and Wings

Cultures—just like parents—give us two things; one is roots and the other is wings.[29] This is a cultural note about Walt and George. Our culture is the madness (from the perspective of others) and the normality (from our perspective) in who we are.

Our roots are in Ohio. Although we did not meet until we were in our thirties (Ah, to be that young again!), the two of us were born less than 20 miles away from each other in northern Ohio, in an area that is sometimes still referred to as The Western Reserve. This strip of northern Ohio along the coast of Lake Erie was first settled by white people toward the end of the 18th century. Many of them (including some of Walt's ancestors) were Puritans and other Protestants from New England who had emigrated from England, Wales, and Scotland during the previous two centuries. Some were seeking religious freedom and others were seeking political or economic freedom.

Those Protestant cultures provided the dominant value system ingested by other European immigrants who came to the Western Reserve in the late 19th and early 20th centuries, such as George's grandparents. So, despite our differences in class, religion, and ethnicity, we are often moved by this common cultural discourse, talking to us from within.

Who We Are (The Madness in our Method)

"Time and tide wait for no man." "A stitch in time saves nine."
"The early bird catches the worm." "Time flies."
"There's no time like the present." "Time is money."
—US cultural discourse, usually served in generous portions with mother's milk.

This could easily be the subject of another book, but for the moment we want to be clear about the value narratives that shaped much of our upbringing and can often be seen as core values in US American life. That is our inherited culture and we do acknowledge it and honor it. That culture is inevitably reflected here, and we want to be conscious about how we use it.

Our wings have taken us elsewhere. So we will also acknowledge the cultures of where we are and where we are going. Because the two of us have been living in different countries and have been plunged in diversity for most of our lives, we regularly find ourselves balancing our original set of cultural values with the rather different cultural values we have now. Like good Scotch whisky, we each began as a single malt—and now we are ageing into a mellow blend. Our cultural values—and the feelings and behaviors that they generate—will emerge as we share our stories.

So, we started out as two Midwestern US white guys from Cleveland, Ohio. Our erratic trajectories through our lives have led us now to George being a US citizen living permanently in France and Walt being a British citizen (campaigning to become a Scottish citizen) living in Scotland. We honor our past and we honor our present as we prepare for our future.

That can be complicated. For instance, Walt would end the previous paragraph by writing "We honour our past" because he honours his present by spelling honour the way people in Scotland do. So although we agree on many things, you will notice that sometimes we go off in very different directions as we speak of our beliefs and values. We hope that encourages you to go in your **own** direction!

I live in the south of France. *Savoir-faire* and *savoir vivre* are core values here. This means knowing how to make your way around by building relationships, and knowing how to enjoy life in ways that have surprisingly made the French, at least according to recent studies, among the most productive people in the world.

So, why France? Time is different here, not less valuable. The pace can be hectic in Paris, but here in Provence life is, as the Irish say, "not a race, but a dance." It takes time and patience to create and nurture friendship and it is richly rewarding. Though the village center is but five minutes away by bike, it can take me the better part of an hour to buy a baguette. It involves saying hello to my barber, a glass of wine offered by Philippe who grills the world's best chicken, a chat with Natalie at the bakery and so on, down the other side of the street on the way home. It's a touch of Bedford, Ohio of the 1940s where I got my small-town start in life.

Why France? At the deepest level, it is the historical, spiritual, and cultural connection between France and grandpa Stanisław's Poland. A master blacksmith conscripted into the Tsar's army, he was fond of reminding us that "Poland was crucified between two thieves." Napoleon was Poland's hope against the neighbors who obsessed and possessed her, and France remained her ideal. On the other side of the family, grandpa Anton never tired of telling of his ancestor, a soldier of Napoleon's invasion, who stayed behind in the retreat.

Why France? I had the best French prof in the world, Hilary Ottensmeyer OSB, affectionately known as Père Hilaire to his students at Saint Meinrad College in southern Indiana. A Sorbonne graduate whose class was anything but conducive to sore buns. He taught not just words, phrases and grammar, but exuded a love of the culture and its literature. I was inspired not just by the poetry of Victor Hugo and Charles Baudelaire, but warmed even more by the songs of Georges Moustaki and Edith Piaf.

Biking from Cleveland to Quebec City was the closest taste I could get for a while. But after a master's program further north in Indiana at L'Université de Notre Dame du Lac,[30] Paris and Deauville[31] became my very first destinations when I was finally able to travel abroad in 1965. It took a long time to percolate, but eighteen years ago, my work, facilitating culture change programs for Ford in Europe, brought me month after month from where I was gloomily living in the Netherlands to the bright little town of La Napoule.[32] I followed my heart and came to stay.

I live in Scotland. Some of our core values are expressed by our national bard, Robert Burns. His verses for *Auld Lang Syne* have spread friendship round the world and his belief that "A man's a man for a' that" keeps us all on the level.[33] Our sense of time here is affected strongly by the weather. If the sun is out, it's time to go for a walk. Now!

Why Scotland? That's a question I'm often asked here, because my American accent has not yet mellowed even after more than thirty years of experiencing the various accents here. The short answer is that I come from Scotland—and from Wales, England, Ireland, and Germany. Those are places from which my ancestors emigrated to America from 1620 onward. They were seeking a place to live that allowed them to live in the way they wanted to live.

I have honored those ancestors by doing exactly the same thing. In 1982, when my life was at a crossroad, I stood on the eastern shore of the USA within a few feet of the Plymouth Rock that commemorates the landing of a group that included one of my own ancestors. I looked across the waves toward Europe and I said aloud: "I'm coming back."

Why Scotland? I went to the same college that my parents did. The College of Wooster was founded by Scottish Presbyterians, the teams are the Fighting Scots, and the football team is led on to the field by a band dressed in MacLeod tartan kilts—with several bagpipers up front. Wooster was where I began losing my Presbyterian religion and where I began recovering my Scottish heritage. When I did my senior thesis in Scottish history, the obvious choice for graduate school was Scotland. I had a wonderful two years in Edinburgh. If I had not met an unusual American woman and followed her back to the US, I would probably have stayed in Scotland. Our divorce thirteen years later freed me to come back.

Why Scotland? Because my love is here. When I first returned to Europe, I lived in London. When I fell in love with Rosie, we attempted to keep my London flat as well as her Scottish home. But the draw of Scotland was stronger. Rosie's two children were in their twenties and warmed my heart by accepting me as step-father. Then when Kathrine was awaiting the birth of her first child, she came into my study and said, "You are going to be Grandpa!" And so I am, now with three wonderful grandchildren. So Scotland is where some of my family of origin came from and Scotland is where my family of choice is now.

On the magical night when we first met—here in Scotland—Rosie and I talked about many things. We discovered that we both have long-ago ancestors from this part of the world and that we share a favorite quotation.[34] T. S. Eliot's wisdom helps us understand how and why a woman born in South Africa and a man born in the US choose to live in Scotland.

We shall not cease from exploration
And the end of all our exploring
Will be to arrive where we started
And know the place for the first time

It took me some time to understand the Scottish question: "Where do you stay?" which means "Where do you live?" It's a very different question from "Where do you come from?"

That is helpful when people discover that I am campaigning for an independent Scotland[35] and wonder about my accent—which still clearly reveals that I was born on the other side of the ocean. I believe what the Yes Campaign says: that decisions about Scotland are best taken by the people of Scotland—the people who live in Scotland. So here is my haiku to shift the focus away from the past to the future:

Where are you from? No.
Ask instead: Where do you stay?
Where are you going?

We invite you, wherever you come from, wherever you are, and wherever you are going, to join us in co-creating our tomorrows.

REFLECTION

What does where you are from tell you about who you are and how you are likely to feel, think, and act? What are your roots and what are your wings as you go for what is next in your life?

While growing up, both of us heard messages from our culture[36] about taking the initiative, taking charge of one's life and career and environments, leveling the playing field, speaking up for what we want and need, taking care of others less fortunate than ourselves, and *time is money.*

It might seem that much of what we are sharing in this book is our own learnings about *saving* precious, perhaps dwindling, time. And it is. But it is also about *savoring* time—in the sense that we are trying to open our later life's days and hours to the doing and enjoying that which is most precious to us. Remember, "Time you enjoy wasting is not wasted time."[37]

We are using our obsession with time to deliver us from it. We are examining how our values interact with each other and challenge us to make choices—so that we can serve the purpose for which we were created: to survive, succeed, and flourish in the environment in which we live, in the age in which we find ourselves, and in the company of those we love and who love us.

Chucket, Ducket, Shucket, and Fucket are not ends in themselves but ways to prepare the space for Plucket, Trucket, and Tucket—in other words, to live well.

So, on with the book!

Small Boy

He picked up a pebble
and threw it into the sea.

And another, and another.
He couldn't stop.

He wasn't trying to fill the sea.
He wasn't trying to empty the
beach.

He was just throwing away,
nothing else but.

Like a kitten playing
he was practising for the
future

when there'll be so many
things
he'll want to throw away

if only his fingers will
unclench
and let them go.

Norman MacCaig[38]

1: The Chucket List

A younger backpacking Walt

Years ago both of us learned to travel lightly as backpackers, enlightened by what became our hiking bible: *The Complete Walker*[39] by Colin Fletcher, who even recommended shortening and drilling out the handle of your toothbrush! Fletcher's dictum was simple: "You look after the ounces and the pounds will look after themselves." So too while wandering through life, as Cesare Pavese put it, "If you wish to travel far and fast, travel light."[40]

However, the little voice that says, "might need that" has often nagged us. When the two of us went to Siberia in 2007 to do a training course on a River Lena cruise ship for our Russian clients, we flew six hours on beyond Moscow with five laptops, five flipchart easels, and several boxes of other training supplies. We were more than a bit embarrassed to read Urszula Muskus in *The Long Bridge* talking about what kept her going during sixteen years in the gulags in the 1940s and 1950s. Her advice on what to take when exiled to Siberia: "something to eat and knitting needles."[41]

Both of us are currently doing lots of Chucket work (clearing our living spaces and working spaces) while we develop our suggestions for you. With luck, some of our ideas will be helpful to you. And, the best Chucket approach will be the one that you create for yourself as you focus on doing it yourself. In the words of Havelock Ellis: "All the art of living lies in a fine mingling of letting go and holding on."[42]

Distasteful as it may at first seem, ageing brings with it a sense of mortality—death feels every day closer than it was yesterday, even though it may be a few decades away. Of course many younger than ourselves will leave life sooner than we do, but it is the awareness that our limited time is passing, not the exact number of years or days that we reckon with. What nicer gift to our heirs than to relieve them of the burden of deciding about what to do with our hoarded junk. We could even give them some of the stuff that we no longer need so they can start using it now.

Chucket Stories: Vanishing space

Cathy and I lived a rather simple life together, early on. As we prospered, we decided to refurnish the bedroom: a new dresser, a 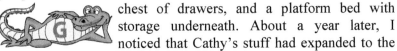 chest of drawers, and a platform bed with storage underneath. About a year later, I noticed that Cathy's stuff had expanded to the point where I was left with only two drawers of my own. For many men, defending a space of their own is not a given. Some years ago one of my men's workshop participants[43] put it this way, "Whether it's the garage or a small room in the basement, you need to establish that it's your space…" Tongue in cheek, he continued, "…even if you need to take your wife and female children to that place and piss in all four corners to mark it as your territory."

Still, things accumulate—even for men. I've been trying to downsize for a long time, not because I need to move anywhere, at least immediately, but because on one hand I'm tired of having to take care of all my junk—most of it really doesn't take care of me. Secondly, like me, much of it has grown old, holds less interest than it used to, so I've gotten in the habit of foisting mementos on visitors. I wonder if it's *Schadenfreude* to be happy about breaking something or losing something—one less thing to care for or worry about.

So even in those moments of accidental breakage and flood damage, momentary regret often yields to a kind of perverse happiness about the loss. It's something about enjoying a new level of freedom.

Chucket is about this reassessment of stuff. Moving can often be the great motivator, when, in later life, you and your partner, if you have one, decide to downsize your living quarters. All too often I hear of individuals or couples who, instead of practicing a bit of Chucket triage before they go, pack it all into the moving van and ship it to the new domicile. Then they struggle for months tripping over boxes and bags whose contents or purpose may even be forgotten.

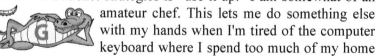

> *REFLECTION*
> *As you look around your space, what kinds of stuff do you see that has become more a burden than an asset?*

Dad's ghost in my kitchen

When you have a lot of something that's doing nothing, one of my favorite eco-Chucket strategies is "use it up." I am somewhat of an amateur chef. This lets me do something else with my hands when I'm tired of the computer keyboard where I spend too much of my home working time. I concoct things in the kitchen. Fridges and cupboards have a way of accumulating things too, sometimes way beyond their expiry date. So, ever so often I go on a rampage to use up the miscellaneous and ageing provisions.

I remember my Dad as a "depression cook," a guy who could make gourmet meals out of the week's remains in the "icebox." (Yes, I'm old enough to remember the iceman feeding it big frozen blocks each week). Often as not, dad supplemented these leftover dibs and dabs with nature's vittles that he would scrounge on a walk in the woods close to our home. Since the fruit does not fall far from the tree, I risk tossing into my recipes a little of this a little of that, in dad's adventurous way. More often than not, the result both surprises and pleases my palate and those of my friends. It can be a bit embarrassing, though, when asked for the recipe!

Wherever your hoard of ageing materiel is stored, kitchen or garage, basement, or under the bed, I suggest that you go and do likewise, asking yourself how can I combine some of this stuff and put it to good use instead of consigning it to a potential eco-hazard.

Chucket strategies
Life is too precious to be possessed by what we possess. So, Chucket is about lightening the load, freeing us from it to do better  things. Enjoy meeting people at your own garage sale before you move, or when you decide to lighten the load. Contribute the no-longer-useful-to-you bits to the local charity or thrift store where they can be of use to someone else. There may be the momentary twinge of loss, but there will also be the joy of giving and a not unbearable lightness of being.

1. Digitizing memories
Memories are an important part of life and identity. When I moved from California to much smaller digs in France, I kept a room in my now-rented house that was a warehouse of memorabilia. File cabinets, bookcases, a trunk, a couple of old suitcases stuffed with my papers, as well as countless photographs that I had taken and been given, family documents, mother's love letters… the list could go on and on. I realized this was storage and not memory. It was too much. Too much to move, too much to have, yet not something I was at all ready to let go of.

Solution? I returned to California over the winter holidays a few years ago, when my house was between renters. I reduced the tangibles by digitizing most of them, scanning photos and documents and posting the originals to other family members and friends who would be the most interested in them. The process took almost two months, twice as long as I had planned. The result? Spectacular! The time-locked memorabilia lost their anonymity and were transformed into real memories. Anything I want to look at became instantly accessible as well as shareable via the Cloud. I can now indulge in and distribute nostalgia at will and without clutter.

Incidentally, reviewing the history of past generations as well as my own history often surprised me. There was stark evidence that parts of stories that I believed and regularly told others didn't pan out when I uncovered and examined the evidence. We tend to construct the identity we think we need, conveniently composing a narrative that involves forgetting what might not quite fit, or simply losing the thread or context of this or that story.

2. Don't set it down someplace, move it on
Years ago, Walt and I designed and taught a course in Time and Life Management in Athens. One of our principal pieces of advice was, "Don't handle anything twice, if you can help it." Back then we were talking mostly about snail mail and paper that overflowed our in-basket, but the advice remains pretty useful in daily life as well. There may be valid reasons for putting things on a shelf for later, but we suggest that you think twice before doing so.

Can I handle it now so I don't have to worry about it later? In my current 55m^2 apartment, I recycle as much as I can as soon as I am done with it. I take satisfaction that my departed stuff, having satisfied my needs, may do something good elsewhere. Many things deserve the deliberate neglect of "out of sight, out of mind." For more about this sense of well-being, see Chapter 7, on Tucket.

Collecting things can also be fun. Some favorites accompany us through life; some need to be laid to rest, because they've served their purpose and now just get in the way. When I was in grade school I started a stamp collection. My dad eagerly encouraged me. It grew and grew. It was a wonderful way to learn geography and geopolitics, though I really didn't know I was doing that at the time.

My collecting served me well. It made me rethink small-town-boy horizons and become more mobile and international. The stamp books and envelopes cluttered my closet for a long time before I realized I would never look at them again. I put them up for sale. Not a great monetary return on the time invested, but the experience of bringing the wide world into my home and my thinking had already paid off big time in other ways. And now, a sigh of relief at the empty shelves. One less thing to own me.

About 15 years ago, in early December, I peeked into a shop in downtown Santa Cruz and saw a ceramic crocodile-shaped lidded casserole. An excellent thing for my coffee table. I could reduce clutter by putting little stuff like keys and matches, etc., into this crockery croc. There was also a little papier-mâché alligator sitting on one of my bookshelves, so I placed it alongside as a fun touch. For Christmas I received five gators from friends. For my birthday a couple weeks later, another half dozen.

Over the years my home became a reptilian bayou with beasts of glass, amber, wire, wood, glass, and even a bright red maraca croc from Cuba. When I was redoing my apartment, I even mused about painting the baseboards in green swamp grass. Not surprisingly, the croc, the god of long life in ancient Egypt, has become my totem. Yet, I was literally up to my derriere in the beasts. Now, I give one away to remember me by, every time somebody admires it or visits me for the first time. See you later alligator!

3. With a little help from Mother Nature
In the fall of 2009 my coastal plain apartment building was inundated by five days of cats-and-dogs rainfall, rising to 1.6 meters in the basement storage area. In France, by the way, the heavens don't pour down domestic pets, but *il pleut comme vache qui pisse.*

Here, "it rains like a cow pisses," a metaphor that says it well, especially if you grew up on or near a farm. In my basement *cave,* I had been storing stuff I no longer had use or room for in my upstairs apartment.

Lo and behold, Mother Nature turned bags and boxes of old docs into papier-mâché and inflicted rot and mildew on most of the rest. I painstakingly photographed it all and let it mold while I sent a claim to the insurance company. Though I got €4000 as an unexpected bonus for my belated and stinking Chucket, it came with the awareness that it might be a lot less hassle to practice Chucket in the here and now rather than schlepp it to the basement of indecision.

4. Does my stuff impose on someone else?

It has been said, "Of the making of books, there is no end."[44] In the course of my studies and dissertation writing at Notre Dame University, I invested in and accumulated hundreds of books—some were commonplace texts, some were quite rare. Only a few of them continued on with me into my work; the rest burdened the floorboards of my mother's attic and her peace of mind for half a dozen years. After far too long I reconciled myself to their departure as a gift, and saw them joyously relieved from my true mater's attic and happily received by my alma mater's library.

Once I passed this first hurdle, the realization grew on me that having lotsa' books was not conducive to my increasingly mobile lifestyle, so I began to conduct regular library purges to benefit good causes. As a reviewer for several intercultural publications, I regularly receive books, read them, scribble about them, and pass them on. My slim home library consists only of the sweetest things, my candy jar of poets and aphorisms, novels and novelties, crunchy literature and history, most of them gonna' reads. A few years ago my music CDs went the way of my books. I iTuned them all and passed out the disks to friends who came to my birthday party.

Today, of course you can kindle the fires of learning and imagination, accessing anything, from anywhere, at any time, as long as the power supply lasts. On the other hand, I do enjoy screen withdrawal, curled up in a comfy place with an old friend whose pages still turn manually.

Back in the pre-digital era, I remember a summer storm power failure, during which my neighbors were astonished to hear arias of the Great Caruso wafting from my windows. Yup, the old hand-cranked Victrola still invited me to put needle to wax and enjoy the sound of nostalgia. So, whether it's cradling a well-worn book spine in my hand or sporting a Hawaiian shirt dating back to the 1970s, it's good to keep a few comfy old things around that still work for you. Even if collecting something is a passion on your bucket list, Chucket still works—get the other stuff out of the way and go for it!

5. Inner and outer ecology

We will be talking more about ways of cleaning up your life in later chapters of this book. It's worth noting here that "stuff" management will not only aid you greatly to do what you want and need to do in life, but ultimately enhance responsible, sustainable living, something our aching world needs you and me to both practice and model. For many of us, it's probably time to say "bye-bye" to buy, buy, buy. As we age and sage, we have the opportunity to become everyday monks and mystics,[45] enjoying simplicity and visiting soul country.

Divorce, Pareto, and Zeno

When I got divorced, I did exactly what George describes above. I moved everything to my new small flat where there was barely enough room for all the boxes. Then I spent several months going through those boxes. This was partly a healing process of crying and of letting go. It was also much, much easier in this new place to know what I no longer needed. Pareto[46] would have been happy: 80% of the stuff in the boxes went to recycling. The 20% that I kept was often valuable—I even found some cash "filed" in a stack of papers.

Months later, I chucked some more things that had become less valuable. Decades later, I'm still chucking some of those once valuable things. Maybe it's like Zeno's paradox.[47] He said that you only get halfway to the goal and then half of that distance—and so on. So each time you Chucket, whether you chuck Pareto's 80% or you chuck Zeno's 50%, at least you can keep on chucking.

As I continue to chuck the things I don't need, I hear the words of Henry David Thoreau[48] urging me to "Simplify, simplify" and that is what I am aiming to do with my stuff and with my life.

Seven Questions to ask when Chucking It

I often create lists of the seven things I have learned about something. Then, rather than preaching my teachings at you, I'm leaning my learnings toward you—as you create your own learnings. My learnings are usually ongoing rather than final. Writing about Chucket is producing learnings learnings both old and new, based both on other's ideas and on my own experiences. Here are the questions that I ask myself as I stand in front of a mound of stuff that is covering my desk so thickly that the desk itself is invisible.

1. Is it useful or beautiful?

As William Morris said, "If you want a golden rule that will fit everybody, this is it: have nothing in your houses that you do not know to be useful, or believe to be beautiful."[49] This simple question condemns a lot of things currently clogging up my study and various other parts of this house. And sometimes this question is enough to get me to chuck it. But if, like me, you have great resistance to chucking stuff, you may need some more questions. The next three come from Stephanie Winston's wonderful book *Getting Organized*.[50] I highly recommend her book if you are getting serious about Chucket.

2. Have I worn it or used it in the past year?

If the answer is yes, says Stephanie Winston, you can keep it. If the answer is no, go to the next question.

My challenge is to be careful with my answer to this one. Sometimes I say to myself that I **might** have worn it or that I **meant** to use it. Those answers count as a no.

3. Does it have value—sentimental or monetary or legal?
This is an interesting one, as David Sparks tells us in his e-book called *Paperless*.[51] When he went through the papers of his parents after they died, the first years of their married life were summarized in one small envelope with a few documents, including a marriage license and a mortgage form. Then organizations started pumping out paper for everything, and the paper from the last years of their lives filled many boxes.

As someone who has checkbooks and expense receipts going back more than fifty years, I'm beginning to accept that even the tax people would never want to see those documents. I suppose part of my problem is that back when I still lived in the US, the Internal Revenue Service once audited me. My accountant told me to take everything to the appointment with the IRS inspector. (She had trained a lot of IRS inspectors so she knew how they would react.)

I remember how the man's eyebrows went up when he called my name and saw me pick up my huge box of files. After twenty minutes or so of asking me for proof of various things—for each of which I then produced evidence—he asked for something that I wasn't sure was actually in the box. But I began looking anyway. "Never mind," he said. "I'm sure it's in there somewhere."

So that has encouraged me to keep everything. But that audit was more than 30 years ago. Most of those files are no longer legally required. And most significantly, I don't need my US files anyway because one of my major Chucket events (although it also qualifies for at least one other list in this book) was my decision to renounce my US citizenship.

The initial trigger was in fact a tax issue. Although the US and the UK have a tax treaty that enables people to pay tax in one country and get credit for it in the other country, the US insisted that I pay taxes that I had already paid the equivalent of in the UK—but not in the same tax year. It took me years to get my money back.

Chucking your taxes or chucking your native country may seem beyond your imagination. But ask yourself why you are a citizen of the country you were born in. As George Bernard Shaw said, "Patriotism is, fundamentally, a conviction that a particular country is the best in the world because you were born in it."[52]

Why do you pay taxes to support wars or policies that you don't believe in? My father was both a lawyer and a peace activist. He sometimes advised people who chose not to pay the portion of their taxes that supported war. He pointed out that this might mean arrest and jail. Some people chose that path; others decided to pay their taxes and protest in other ways.

The last minutes of the film *American Graffiti* always make me cry. The film's advertising line was "Where were you in '62?" I was graduating from high school—like the people in that film. And my classmates made 60s choices similar to the choices of the characters in the film: going to Vietnam and coming back changed—or not coming back, going to college to avoid the draft, moving to Canada, settling down in the hometown as an insurance agent. We all chucked a lot of dreams in those years. And now we are chucking paper that reminds us of those dreams.

There is a simple secret for chucking paper. As David Sparks (who is a lawyer) says in *Paperless*, if I really want to keep it I can scan it onto a hard drive and shred the paper. Most documents don't need to be kept for more than seven years; check your local legal requirements with a lawyer and an accountant. We could all probably go back to that one envelope of really important papers.

The other part of Stephanie Winston's question is about sentimental value, and the key word is *real* sentimental value. If I can't remember who gave me this souvenir or I can't remember why I got it for myself, then it no longer has sentimental value. If you can convince yourself that something has legal or sentimental value, then Stephanie Winston says you can keep it. If the answer is no, go to the next question.

4. Might it come in handy some day?
If the answer, says Stephanie Winston, is yes, it might come in handy some day—then THROW IT OUT! Let me repeat that, because it is so difficult for me (and people like me). You ask yourself the question: Might it come in handy some day? You answer yourself: Yes. And then you throw it out! So, yes or no, you **throw it out**.

I love that. So I've got Winston's three questions posted on signs in my cupboards, in my garage, and here in my study. I've had them up for years—since soon after I first read her book in 1978. Her point is simple. Even if very occasionally I chuck out something that I do need later, I can always get a replacement. But almost everything else I will NOT need.

My only problem with this wonderful question is that after 35 years I have built up a lot of resistance to it. So I have added three more questions that I learned from three other people.

5. Could someone else make better use of this?
When my parents decided to sell the house in which they had raised their five children, we five were all very reluctant to see that happen. Dad's response was simple: "You enjoyed reading in the attic, swinging on the porch, playing baseball and other games in and around this house; it's time to give that chance to other young children." This question has helped me a lot in the last couple of years as I have struggled to clear some space on my bookshelves. Much as I love to have all these books, I have finally accepted that I will never read some of them, that having

three copies of one book is more than enough, and that re-reading some books for a fourth time is not really necessary.

This also helps with clothes and other small items, but it really got going when I was using lots of supplies for my training courses. I would come home with leftover markers, sticky notes, pens, pencils, and other things. A friend of ours was a teacher in a primary school in a nearby village and when I offered her a few items, she accepted enthusiastically—and asked for more.

That went on for several years and I even got the reward of being invited to the Christmas pageant. When our friend retired, she suggested I transfer my donations to the primary school here in our own village. In addition to lots of stationery supplies, I have also donated four laptop computers—and had the joy of helping twelve-year-olds learn to make movies with them. As my father once said when thanked for all his gifts to the college, "There is something in the air of Wooster that transmutes giving into receiving." That is how I feel about the air in our village too.

6. Have you applied the Benedictine Rule?
Several years ago, I came across a wee book that suggested ways to apply the ancient *Rule of St. Benedict* to modern life.[53] One point is brilliantly simple: it is okay to buy a new shirt, a new book, or a new electronic gadget—as long as I give away an old shirt, book, or gadget. That means that the pile of stuff does not get any bigger!

7. And what else?
This was the question I learned from Rosie when we first met. It applies in various ways to various situations. Here, it is a very simple and very final question: And what else could I chuck out? What if I chucked out just *one more thing* each time I got going? I could do my own version of Columbo.[54] Instead of coming back in the door as the detective to ask the suspect *just one more thing*, I could come back to a stack of useless stuff and say to myself: "Just one more thing." And then throw out that extra

thing too! I've just come up with this idea while writing about Chucket—so I will pause here to experiment with it. Onward—and *outward*!

A Conversation
Wanderer to Hermit: "You have so little in your hut."
Hermit to Wanderer: "And you have so little on your back."
Wanderer to Hermit: "But I'm just passing through."
Hermit to Wanderer: "And so am I."

A sample Chucket List

If you are wondering what your Chucket List might look like, here is the latest version of my own Chucket List to give you an example:

Shred all receipts and invoices dated earlier than 2010
Give away old glasses for re-use in other parts of the world
Donate old computer stuff to local college's repair project
Give away old file cabinets in the garage—after shredding the files!

Chucket hints

Chucket is not a onetime thing. You may want to make an actual list if you are involved in a specific effort to trim down your current clutter, move to a new residence, remodel, etc. Of course, if these are not on your agenda, spring-cleaning (or you pick the season) is an option, and will go well with humming a freedom song...

However, Chucket is a frame of mind worth developing. Make a habit of asking yourself the question, "Should I chuck it?" Then use Walt's questions to decide. We would highly recommend that after your initial chucking adventures, you keep a Chucket poster or a to-do list visible where it will stimulate you to property slimming.

The need for Chucket may seem a reaction to a society of superabundance, but in fact hoarding may be more common when and where there is less, so one becomes less discriminating when it comes to what to save and what to chuck. My parents were a Great Depression couple, who kept rather than trashed anything that might be remotely useful.

When my grandfather, a real do-it-all Mister Fixit, came to live with us, our basement became his workshop and storage spaces were crammed with potential raw material solutions for unspecified problems. Bottles of nails and screws hung from the rafters; bricks, beams and scrap iron were hidden under the porch. My parents inherited the lot on Grandpa's death and had not quite disposed of it by the time they had both passed away. My cousins and I were the not-so-delighted heirs and executors of two generations of stuff.

Our consumerist society has too long advocated replace over repair, though repeating economic crises may dictate for some a return to the former. Darning socks may not be your forte, but do consider that some fix-its may serve you and your world in many cases better than the minuscule eco-tax on discarded electronics.

Does the challenge look too big? Sometimes I put off chucking something because it's too big, too heavy, or I just don't know what to do with it. But I can ask family or friends or experts on the web to get the help I need, whether information or extra hands.

Chucket does not always mean throw it in the trash, but rather *to reroute it in a responsible way*. Sometimes this may be the nearest recycling bin, but often it means reviewing options like those on the checklist below to decide whether and how to Chucket.

Should I Chucket or not?
Here are some criteria to add to Walt's list of seven that may help you create a process for things you are still uncertain about.

❑ It's clearly mine to keep or dispose of.
❑ It does not promote personal, familial, or social well being as I see it if I keep it.
❑ It is not a personal or familial, symbol or memory.

❏ I cannot presently or shortly put it into service in a useful way.
❏ It's taking up space I need or could use for something else.
❏ It doesn't provide backup to something essential that I have just replaced.
❏ It doesn't represent the art or effort of someone who would be sensitive to my letting go of it.
❏ I don't know what it is or where it came from, nor can anyone else tell me.

How to Chucket

Of course, one way to chuck something may be to just shitcan it! However, with ecological sensitivity, that now means recycle it or its components. If it seems too good to just trash, you can:

- Hold a garage sale or flea market event of your own, or share such an event with the neighbors. "One man's junk is another man's treasure!"
- Amazon it or eBay it. Sell it or trade it for something else you really need.
- Give it to someone who needs it, likes it, who has expressed an interest in it, or who will appreciate the gesture.
- Donate it to your local thrift shop or charity. In many places there are now shops or markets open daily where people regularly both buy and sell used but usable items—and in other areas there are local websites to facilitate this process.
- Keep it, but rearrange or reemploy it in a way that it actively contributes to your environment and those in it. Environmentally conscious folks are often creating both marvelously artful as well as useful and practical things out of plastic bags and even  road-worn tires. No bull! Yes, a rubber-tired but not tired-looking bull. We saw it at an art exhibit a few months ago…
- **Celebrate your Chucket success with a Tucket!**

To attain knowledge, add something every day.
To attain wisdom, remove something every day.

Lao Tzu[55]

2: The Shucket List

We both grew up in northern Ohio in the US, where the sweet corn was a gourmet vittle— but, we had to shuck it. That meant ridding the ear of husk and silk before the water boiled. When you roasted corn on an open fire, shucking the charred ear was finger-singeing work. In the days when food did not come pre-shucked in plastic, it took shucking, shelling, and peeling to get to the good stuff. Pit the cherries, shuck the peas, peel the onions, unstring the string beans.

George had to scale the pike and gut the perch that his Dad had hooked out on Lake Erie. He even had the rather lugubrious delight of pulling the feathers from the chicken, goose, or duck that his Grandmother Barbara had brought to an inglorious end with a quick twist of the wrist, out of sight of the children in the basement, while Walt pulled feathers from a chicken that his grandfather had brought to an even quicker demise down at the chicken coop, with a hatchet. Once seen—never forgotten. The best down got sorted and saved so George could sleep with birdie ghosts of yesteryear stuffed in the coverlets and pillows sewn by Grandma and Aunt Kate.

Perhaps it's due to all that corn picking and corn shucking that both of us have a penchant for corny humor. Although we've both been significantly over-educated, even when we pull off a multilingual pun with a reference to a modern poet or an ancient playwright, it can still sound corny.

Feel free to ignore our corny references and our corny jokes—shuck them off and we still think you'll find something good inside. If not, well, shucks, man. We tried!

Shucket: Get to the heart of the matter.

Peel off the unneeded, the distracting, the useless. Shucking is not chucking. It is usually a bit more work. It may be taxing or tedious at first, but it is necessary and ultimately gratifying when we bring clean results to the table of life. Shucking may surprise us by revealing a feast that has been imprisoned by the husks of the superfluous.

Not all Shucket is physical—much of it is in the head and the heart, as Walt says below in a grook—a playful kind of poetry invented by Piet Hein.[56]

Sometimes I tidy my shelf
Sometimes I tidy my self
Tidying outside stuff is shelfish
Tidying inside stuff is selfish

But sometimes I tell my self
To focus on self instead of shelf
It's not enough to clear our shelves
We need to clear our selves

Things are not what they seem

Pulling off the husks from everyday nostrums or "accepted wisdom" for the first time may bring to light shining realities that 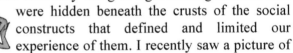 were hidden beneath the crusts of the social constructs that defined and limited our experience of them. I recently saw a picture of a mirror, with a note attached to it that read, "Reflections in this mirror may be distorted by socially constructed ideas of 'beauty'." In other words, even my self-image, my self-acceptance, can be distorted by commonly accepted judgments in my culture or group, or by the way that the products that are supposed to make me look good are marketed.

A recent cartoon showed a woman asking a man, "Do I look fat?" His mumbled response: "Do I look crazy?" Beauty is often suffocated by its clothing and there is a price to be paid sometime for revealing it, for telling the truth.

Someone once said, "All art is obscene." The author meant that in the etymological sense of the word. *Skene*, in Greek, is the tent cloth that hides something within. Good art pulls off the wrappings of the everyday in such a way as to unclothe its true shape, form, beauty. I can't visit Disneyland without going away with the song line, "Everything is beautiful in its own way..." repeating itself in my head. Shucket is finding my way back to basics.

Talmudic traditions argue over the nature of the Klippoth, shells that encase and hide sparks of divine power but which need to be broken open for creative energy to be released. As one master put it, it is the responsibility of each human being to deal with whatever comes to him or her in life, creation and its creatures, in such a way that the light and beauty and possibilities contained may be revealed and released. Taking this philosophy to heart, Shucket becomes the modus operandi of the enlightened man, the artist at life, whatever the faith that guides him to it.

When we introduced Chucket, we quoted the Italian poet Cesare Pavese to say, "If you wish to travel far and fast, travel light." Yup, we need to keep the pounds and ounces of material reality from holding us back, but even more importantly, as Pavese puts it in the next line, there are other kilos and grams that can be even more weighty:

"Take off all your envies, jealousies, unforgiveness, selfishness and fears... the closing years of life are like the end of a masquerade party, when the masks are dropped. "[57]

Shucket!

REFLECTION
What of my old attitudes, worldviews, thinking patterns need cleaning up? What beliefs or mindsets help you go beneath the surface and see what you may have missed?

 # Further Reflections on Shucket

Shucking off fears of the unfamiliar
What you see or find, what life brings you today may be new, different, and not be easy to grasp or use, but it is the real thing. My dad used to say, "Suck it. If you've lost all your teeth (as he had), gum it to death!" Shucket is abetted by curiosity and courage.

I was blessed to have a great mentor in my father. He was a sport fisherman on his days off. Sometimes that meant fly-casting for crappies or trout in Tinkers Creek near our Bedford, Ohio home. More often, though, it meant a car trip to Edgewater Harbor where Dad kept a small boat for fishing on Lake Erie. On the way home, he would regularly take me to dinner in a different nationality restaurant. Cleveland in those days harbored at least 50 different ethnic neighborhoods, so there was never a shortage of possibilities.

Dad's motto was, "Try anything twice...the first time could have been a fluke." He left me with a lifelong curiosity about people, culture, and life, not just about food. Even today, though, when I find myself in a foreign environment, I will pick stuff off the menu that I haven't heard of, sometimes to the bewilderment of the waiter, given the combinations I'm choosing. Shucking off fear opens the soul to curiosity and adventure.

Shuck "beginning of the end" thinking
I awoke with a headache this morning. It turned out not to be a stroke. Breakfast disappeared it. It is all too easy as we age to spend our time wondering if our aches and pains, discomforts and missteps are "the beginning of the end." A headache, a sore throat, a stomach upset, an unfamiliar twinge here or there and the worries sprout. Shucket is a handy way to remember to strip these things down to what they are and nothing more until we have solid evidence to the contrary.

If whatever it is doesn't go away in a short while, see the doctor and get the facts and the remedies. Choose your doctors well for their clinical skills or their bedside manner—whichever feels most reassuring to you. Beatrice Cheviron, my GP, deals and heals both with facts and fun. Just walking through the door of her waiting room I feel better already. After she wrote a Rx for my touch of flatulence the other day, I told her I was on my way to working in Turkmenistan and jokingly asked her if she wanted me to bring her anything from there. "Yes," she quipped, "a large canister of bottled gas." Your doctor can help you Shucket.

"The beginning of the end" occurred on the day I was born. I survived diaper rash, allergies, premature weaning, chicken pox, zits, dietary religions, dental visits, school exams, job changes, the comings and goings of people in my life—all the bumps in the road that have brought me to where I am now.

I am learning to shuck all too common cautions and stereotypes about debilitating old age. They can become disabilities in their own right. When I leave the house forgetting the grocery list, I can blame my deteriorating memory, suspect the onset of Alzheimer's, and consign myself to feeling much more inadequate than I am. Or…, I can remember my mother chiding me at age 18 when I returned from the corner store without something or other, "You'd forget your head if it wasn't attached."

Worldviews askew

It is far too large a subject for a deep look here, but we may even have to learn how to shuck off worldviews that our kind has spun off as true, but are either not working or may be working against us. What have I been sold and told by politicos, demagogues, and marketers claiming to explain who I am and what I need and who I should dislike or even eliminate? Would-be puppeteers can now chase me down via my handheld devices to keep their claims and offers before my eyes and echoing in my ears. Spying isn't new. It has just become more efficient at getting into my head and learning my habits.

Is there an escape from these gated worlds? Meditation and reflection are age-old antidotes. They help me see the relativity and fabricated nature of what would pose as reality. They keep me from drinking the Kool-Aid when some constructed world starts to fall apart. Whether I sit in the lotus position (hard to do these days), chant like a monk, whirl like a Sufi dervish and spin off poetry, kneel in my church or your mosque or just go fishing, I can start to recognize the illusions.

The French have a saying, *Plus ça change, plus c'est la même chose.* (The more things change, the more they stay the same). This suggests a close look at what I hold in my hands, head, or heart so I can shuck off the illusionary husks and novel labels that may keep me clinging to a same-old same-old that is no longer relevant.

REFLECTION
What unfamiliar things in my surroundings might I want to take a deeper look at? What sorts of people do I tend to dismiss without trying to understand them?

Clean up your language

Shucket can also be a matter of language. This is not just about political correctness or prudery, but paying attention. As Australians are wont to remind us, sometimes I gotta, "Call a spade a bloody shovel!" at least admitting to myself what it really is for me. I need to pay attention to the rape of language in governmental and organizational politics, where CYA ("cover your backside" behavior) dominates and where *Amtsprache* covers its sins. *Amtsprache* was the bureaucratic language that Nazi officers said made atrocities easy. "Not my fault." "Just following orders." "It's policy…" "Just doing as I was told."

Likewise in advertising. Consumer-attractive packaging can be higher on the agenda than quality content. Advertisers were taught, "to sell the sizzle, not the steak," long before they started merchandising spam. I learned about how important it was to shuck language because of the upchuck I experienced when Richard

Nixon, attempting to cover up Watergate, declared that his previous statements were "inoperative." Politicians are inclined to "misspeak" rather than "lie" and to cover over the blood and guts in the street as "collateral damage." Two traditional roles for guys are those of "sage" and "protector." I can exercise these roles today, more than ever before, by looking wisely at the stories I am told and by alerting myself and others not to step into what male bovines leave behind on TV and in our handheld devices.

Don't get me wrong, I've nothing against politeness or artful seduction, and, as a professional working interculturally, I am fully aware of the convenient distinction made between "direct" and "indirect" communication styles and the dangers of stereotypes. I observe that we more direct folks tend to interpret more indirect folks as befuddlers or as deliberately hiding something, if not lying to us. People in the same culture as the speaker understand quite well what he or she has in mind—I am the one who needs to Shucket. To me the essence of politeness is goodwill served warm or on ice as the cultural recipe may demand. "Telling it like it is" is best done according to the mores of where I find myself.

REFLECTION
Where and with whom (including myself) am I reluctant to or confused about how to "tell it like it is"?

Harbor no regrets

"A thousand memories and not a single regret"
Edgar Lee Masters[58]

One of my all time favorite songs is Edith Piaf's *"Non, Je ne regrette rien."* (No, I don't regret anything).[59] She sings:

>*Ni le bien qu'on m'a fait*
>(Not the good things that have been done to me)
>*Ni le mal tout ca m'est bien egal*
>(Nor the bad things, I shrug them all off)

C'est payé, balayé, oublié
(It's paid for, swept away, forgotten)
Je me fous du passé
(I don't give a damn about the past)

The root of the word "regret" actually means, "to lament all over again." Once regret sets in, it can invade my life with a recurring and paralyzing misery. Some people spend a lifetime bemoaning and complaining about what happened way back when. Dr. Gordon Livingstone suggests that there should be a figurative statute of limitations on childhood traumas.[60]

So too, for later hurts and self-reproaches. So to the question, "What do you regret…?" I have two possible responses, either shuck it, get to the heart of the matter and if I can still pursue what I missed or miffed, put it on my bucket list, if I think it can still be done and is worth doing. Or, I can simply say, "Aw shucks," and chuck it and get on with life. After all, as Rumi reminds us, "If you are irritated by every rub, how will your mirror be polished?"[61]

Seven Shucket Learnings

1. The Past
I've been fascinated by the past all my life. Our summer trips as a family included visits to battlefields and other historical sites. We even took a "Lincoln trip" to visit the birthplace and other important locations in Lincoln's life. If there was an historical marker beside the highway, we pulled off to read it. So it's not surprising that like my two older sisters, I majored in history. I then went on to get a master's degree in Scottish History by coming up with a new theory of a battle that took place in 1650.

In recent years, I've reviewed my view of that battle and have gradually shucked my conviction that my hero—the Marquis of Montrose—was on the "right side" back in the 17th century.[62] My sense now is that the clans up on the hill (who did not join the battle until they could see which group of outsiders was winning) were the important ones. They were protecting their homes and their families.

It took me decades to shuck my view of the hero I was writing about. I'm no longer so impressed by his brilliant strategies or his string of military victories. Shucking the need for well-intentioned military interventions in distant places is a long, slow process that many of us still struggle with today. What I now honor, after nearly fifty years of shucking the stuff about his military exploits, is the core of Montrose: an inspiring poet and activist who—while surrounded by extremists—took enthusiastic action in support of the middle ground.

The past is full of people and events that are worth honoring—and it may take lots of shucking to find the core. When I was doing my research on Montrose, I went into a room at Register House in Edinburgh where one man was painstakingly cataloguing the papers of the Graham family—Montrose began life as James Graham. The boxes of papers in that room soared toward the ceiling in crazy stacks that Dr. Seuss would have loved.

The cataloging man found a box of papers from the mid-seventeenth century. Looking through the box, I found a piece of parchment signed by Montrose himself. It was a memorable moment. But the piece of paper that earned me my degree was another letter that I found in the National Library of Scotland. Shucking the long pages down to the core, I found a statement by one of the losers about how the battle had happened. History is too often written by the winners—and that is only half of history.

As anyone who knows the true history of Macbeth can tell you, he was one of Scotland's more successful and long-reigning kings. But Shakespeare wrote his play based on history written by the winners. Such history needs to be shucked at the least. And maybe even chucked!

Even if you're not interested in Scottish history, you do have your own history and the history of your family. Recently I went with four other old guys to see a performance of Eugene O'Neill's play *Long Day's Journey into Night*. This is an autobiographical play that O'Neill described as "this play of old sorrow, written in tears and blood."[63]

When I first saw this play many years ago, I identified with the young man (based on O'Neill himself) who has confrontations with his mother, with his father, and with his brother. The facts are totally different from my own family history, and yet the feelings are very familiar—in both senses of the word. This time I found myself identifying with the old man—and being startled to realize that the character is younger than I am now.

In the play—and in real life—the father made some choices that remind me of choices I have made. Rather than losing myself in drink or depression as the character does, my ongoing learning about my past is to shuck those temptations and those past pains so that I can move on. As a wise person once told me, it's never too late to have had a happy childhood.

And now I've decided it's never too late to have a happy adulthood. As I was contemplating a second marriage, my friend Ed Mayhew told me he had gone into his second marriage saying to himself: "If anyone is going to be unhappy in this marriage, it isn't going to be me." That has been a very helpful reminder over the years—not only about marriage, but also about life in general.

Unlike shucking an ear of corn, shucking the past can be a repetitive process. I need to shuck the history that other people tell me about world events, so that I don't get misled by old propaganda. I need to shuck the history that I tell myself about personal events, so that I don't get distracted by old myths about myself. As the updated saying goes, it's bad enough to put old wine in new bottles, but taking old whine into new battles is even more risky. Some memories need to be shucked again and again to remove the painful outsides so that I can treasure the beauty at the core.

2. The Future

I've been fascinated by the future all my life. As Kettering said, "I'm interested in the future because I'm going to spend the rest of my life there."[64] One way I focus on the future is by reading science fiction. I've recently been re-reading a collection of top science fiction stories from the 1940s and 1950s—and reading about things like isolation via virtual reality, VOIP communication, and drones. These stories of the future were written so long ago that they call a television a "televisor" and they refer to certain people in no-longer-acceptable language. But when I shuck those terms and those expressions, then the core of the story still reveals inspiring possibilities for how I can live my life more effectively.

A powerful description of how we can shuck our self-limiting beliefs comes from a science fiction novel by Orson Scott Card called *Speaker for the Dead*:

> *The difference between [human] and [alien] is not in the creature judged, but in the creature judging. When we declare an alien species to be [human], it does not mean that they have passed a threshold of moral maturity. It means that we have.*[65]

So when I shuck my racist or sexist beliefs about someone, it does not mean that they have changed. I am the one who has changed—and needs to keep on changing. As part of my continuing work on myself in relation to others, I've developed seven learnings about diversity[66] that continue to guide me and challenge me. As with the past, the shucking of self-limiting beliefs about the future and about others is an iterative process.

Although we lost the referendum in September 2014, I'm still involved in the ongoing campaign for Scottish independence. Even after four years of campaigning, I'm still fascinated by all the different issues that people discuss—from the economy to identity to defense to education. Reading what people write about these ongoing issues requires a tremendous amount of shucking to get to the core message. My sense is that the difference between those who will vote Yes next time and those who will vote No can be shucked down to this core: NO is about fear, problems, and the past while YES is about hope, possibilities, and the future.

As each of us as individuals, let alone as nations, grows up and moves away from dependence to independence—and then moves into the ultimate interdependence of equals—we do better when we focus on hope instead of fear, possibilities instead of problems, and the future instead of the past. Shucking the negative three opens up the positive three.

3. The Present
And I've been fascinated by the present all my life. My original training at the Gestalt Institute of Cleveland helped me learn to focus on here and now. That is very difficult, because thoughts of the past and thoughts of the future distract me from the present.

It can be as simple as paying attention. Perhaps by looking up from my keyboard to look out the window of this speeding train in which I am writing today—and see a delightfully multi-colored spinning ball out in the middle of a field among other scarecrows.

When I am working with a group, my task is to shuck thinking about what just happened or imagining what might happen next. My task is to pay attention in the present, to notice what is.

Paying attention is simple—but not easy. There is a distinction between those two words: simple and easy. Marriage and world peace are both simple. Neither is easy. But shucking the tons of stuff that surrounds each one is a way to get to the core of marriage and the core of world peace. And shucking the tons of stuff that distracts me from the present moment is a way to get to the core of what is happening now—so I can notice it and even enjoy it.

4. The Stuff

When my young grandson Eric receives a gift for his birthday, he does not pause to examine the lovely wrapping paper or even the box with the pictures of what is inside. He rips off the paper, tears open the box, and grabs the toy itself! Eric has shucked what is not needed so he can enjoy the core. Like the small boy in Norman MacCaig's poem (at the beginning of Chapter 1), he is learning to shuck in a way that he can continue using throughout his life.

Some stuff that surrounds me needs the Chucket approach. But other stuff is like my grandson's gift. Deep inside there is something worth keeping. Although much of what we have been talking about is what to get rid of, there are also things worth keeping.

When my Aunt Sarah died at 98, I spoke at her funeral. I spoke of her as a Keeper. She was a keeper of birthdays (she sent thousands of birthday cards), a keeper of books (always hardbacks, as the devoted librarian she was), a keeper of the library, a keeper of community, a keeper of the family, a keeper of the house, and a keeper of Christmas. I learned a lot from Aunt Sarah about how to keep—and what to keep.

The choice is often between Keep and Change—and as my friend Marianne Erdelyi says, the one who chooses to keep often makes it possible for another to choose to change. So as I look at the stuff I have, I do choose to keep some of it. But other stuff I choose to let go of so that I have time and energy to **keep** those other important things like the community and the family.

When I'm choosing what to keep, I can now also choose how to keep it. Neil, my stepson, has transformed all my records and tapes into electronic versions that exist only on disk and in something called a cloud! Stuart, my stepdaughter's partner, has transformed thousands of slides and photos into electronic versions. Next come the old videotapes—so the Shucket process sometimes involves removing the husk of photo album or audiotape to preserve only the dancing electrons that reproduce the image or the sound.

5. The Talk

I get paid for telling stories. I tell them on my training courses and I tell them in my writings. One key to a good story is to shuck the parts of the story that confuse people and don't support the point of the story. Years ago, a friend told me that she wasn't listening to me because I kept telling two background stories before I got to the important story. So now (at least some of the time) I shuck the background stories and go straight to the core story. The book that I wrote on influencing has more than a hundred stories—and I shucked each one a bit (or a lot) to emphasize the core.

The discipline—as I get older—is to avoid being a garrulous (wonderful word) old man who has, as someone wrote recently of a character, replaced conversation with lectures. And one way I get good stories is to be quiet long enough to hear other's stories. Have I told you the story of the man from WFP (the UN World Food Programme) who told a group of us in Darfur how he was delivering food to a remote village when his truck broke down, so he negotiated with someone to borrow some camels—and successfully delivered the food? Yes, I've told you just now, having shucked the details to give you the essence of a courageous man's amazing story.

When Rosie and I got married (George was one of the celebrants!) we shucked a lot of the traditional wedding service so that it suited both of us. Rosie and I wrote our own vows. Each of us said to the other, "I promise to love you, trust you, and cherish you for the rest of my life." Cherishing is the gift of loving and trusting—not just in the way I want to love and trust, but also in the way that you want to be loved and trusted.

My own Shucket challenge is to let go (at least sometimes) of how I want to be cherished—and instead to notice the taste of homemade bread, to notice the holiday that has been carefully planned, to notice my favorite blueberries appearing in the fridge, and to notice again the lovely grin that I first fell in love with.

Raymond Carver gradually shucked more and more words so that his late writings used very few words—and went straight to the core. His poem called *Late Fragment*[67] is about a very special gift:

And did you get what you wanted from this life, even so?
I did.
And what did you want?
To call myself beloved, to feel myself beloved on this earth.

6. The Silence

I also get paid to shut up. When I'm facilitating a T Group,[68] I say to each of the dozen or so people sitting in a circle with me: "Your task is to learn about yourself, about each other, and about groups— by doing whatever we do." Then I shut up. When I'm doing process consulting with the top team of an organization, I tell them I'm there to listen and perhaps offer observations later. Then I shut up. In both cases, I continuously shuck my temptations to speak and my temptations to think about what's going on. Instead I focus my attention on noticing (not interpreting, just noticing) what I see, what I hear, and what I feel as I sit with the group. It may look like doing nothing, but it's the most intense work that I do.

Like the three princes of Serendib, who were "always making discoveries, by accidents and sagacity, of things which they were not in quest of," I find that by shucking other distractions, I can combine what I notice by chance with the wisdom gained from experience. That leads to interventions that others find helpful.

Forty years ago, I got a blunt version of the wisdom of shutting up. I was working with Herb Shepard, one of the creators of Organization Development[69] as a profession. Herb kindly agreed to co-lead two weekend workshops with me and I was eagerly watching him so I could learn from the master. By Saturday evening of the first workshop, Herb had made only two or three interventions. So I asked him over dinner why he wasn't saying more. Herb leaned back in his chair, sipped at his white wine, and said: "Walt, if you had fucked up as many interventions as I have, you'd be quiet too."

7. The Art

Picasso says, "Art is the elimination of the unnecessary."[70] Giorgio Vasari described sculpting done by Michelangelo as a process of removing the marble that was not part of the statue.[71] Michelangelo took a hammer to a fifteen-foot-tall block of marble and shucked the bits that were not David. Imagine a long, happy life of all sorts of possibilities. Take a hammer and shuck the bits that are not you.

"Less is more." [72] Whether sculpting or painting or creating anything—and even when appreciating someone else's creation—what is left out allows what is important, useful, and beautiful to emerge. So, too with the lives we sculpt for ourselves. Chucket and Shucket are two chisels in your art-of-living toolbox as you sculpt the masterwork which is you. There are more chisels to come.

And if you are still learning to use those chisels like Michelangelo,[73] I offer you some wisdom from Lily, my granddaughter. She is now a teenager but I have been watching her draw since she was small. She draws a lot. When some of her friends asked her how she got to be so good at drawing, Lily replied by saying something like this: *Get a sketchbook. Fill it. Copy good artists. Keep practicing. Get another sketchbook. Fill it again. Keep drawing.*

A sample Shucket List

If you are wondering what your Shucket List might look like, here is the latest version of my own Shucket List to give you an example:

Shuck the articles ripped from magazines; scan some, then chuck all
Shuck the boxes of training materials; donate stuff to the school
Shuck, scan, then chuck the files of family letters and friend letters
Shuck each file folder each time I put something into it

> *REFLECTION*
> *What mindsets (about past, present, and future) do I need to shuck—or keep—to sculpt my own personal masterpiece?*

Look on every exit being an entrance somewhere else.

Tom Stoppard[74]

3: The Ducket List

Ducket is a way to avoid commitments and obligations sent flying in your direction, especially when those commitments or obligations don't match your own sense of contribution to your family and community or don't fit with your own needs and your own sense of who you are. We are not refusing to be stretched by new challenges and opportunities, but as we age we get more alert to what will work and what won't, so that indiscriminate demands don't distract us from what we can best continue to give and do.

Sometimes we may say yes to what others ask because, in what seems like a shrinking world (with friends disappearing and the days going by more quickly), we can become eager to be connected with others, to be noticed, and to be part of what is going on. Not a bad thing in itself, but much better if what we accept being a part of really fits what we can and want to bring to it. Saying *yes* out of neediness, when *no* would be much more to everyone's benefit, serves neither them nor us. It may be more useful to duck even the idea of waiting to be asked; instead, ask people to join you in doing what you want to do!

Ducket is not an invitation to isolation or loneliness; rather it is an invitation to focus on what you really want to do for yourself as well as with and for others—rather than be distracted by other requests. As we will say again in the Trucket chapter, we believe there is lots to do in the world, including such things as generously using your time to support and mentor another generation.

Ducking it

For well over a quarter of a century now, I have been a very active member of a voluntary professional organization of interculturalists called SIETAR[75] in which I am seen by quite a few who don't know any better as a bit of an *éminence grise*. A recent social network study, using a software system called Connection Scan,[76] plotted me at dead center in this organization's communications exchange network.

While I feel good about being well known and respected, and enjoy mentoring younger people in my field, this was scary evidence that my celebrity and seniority in that small circle sets me up as the target of calls and emails which assume that I am the source of all information and can make just about anything happen. They come to me first instead of to the secretary or the appropriate committee, often even when the inquirer could find what they needed to know on the organization's website or just Google it.

Because of my interest in the people and the work, it would be easy to build my *Macher* image in both the positive "doer" and negative "manipulator" sense of that Yiddish word. I choose to respond with politeness, give quick but correct references to what, where, and from whom to find help or solutions, realizing that to do less would be discouraging to the inquirer, while to do much more would overwhelm and overpower me as well as disempower others in their responsibilities.

Good delegation is part of Ducket. It is not avoiding the person or the issue, but responsibly pointing people to appropriate, even better, resources—thus also empowering up-and-coming colleagues.

Some people enjoy "throwing their weight around." Now that I have considerably more weight (avoirdupois as well as influence), it's harder to throw it around! Having it brings the awareness that I don't have to throw it around; I just have to realize its uses and limitations and employ it where it fits and share it calmly and well.

When I Ducket, I can pass on opportunity in such a way that someone else can be enabled to sprout, grow, and bloom.

Just 'cuz everybody else is doing it...

Dads, mums, and teachers are often quick to counsel their grade-schoolers, "Just because everybody else is doing it, it doesn't mean you have to do it too." Some of the demands that play on me have to do with standards, possessions, clothing, appearance, and behaviors I am implicitly but repeatedly urged to accept.

When I'm getting ready to go out on a rainy day, I can still hear my mother's voice reminding me "wear your rubbers" (common term for gumshoes then, not condoms). Cultural norms and expected behaviors are often repeatedly imposed on me explicitly or implicitly and willy-nilly continue to prompt me from within. There is often a price to pay for non-compliance; yet, compliance may extort even more from my health and vitality.

Here are two examples, one about gender and the other about age.

If I fail to nail a male tale, will I wind up in jail and never make bail?

Neither of us is a gay guy, but we can be pained and constrained as well by other people's definitions of "what it takes to be a man." If you happen to be a gay guy, you know this pressure far better than we do. The culture I grew up in put a premium on men being active and productive, always busy about doing or making something. I grew up with a maxim, "Idleness is the devil's workshop," ringing in my ears, so it was easy to feel compelled when relaxation was interrupted with, "Why don't you...?"

Watching the footie on TV with ale in hand too easily invites interruption, so guys also invented sport fishing. Under the guise of providing seafood for dinner, fishing offers quiet moments by the water, occasionally interrupted by a nibble and a catch and a sip of something warming. It was Brother David Steindl-Rast[77] who even suggested that, for the sake of our spirit, we might sometimes decide to cast the line without baiting the hook. One can always buy a few fish at the market on the way home as long as you put them in your creel and are careful to discard the price tags.

Act your age!
This is also a reproach for kids, but, in fact, it shows up again at least by implication on the other end of life. While I was taking a dip in our residence swimming pool, my neighbor Henri swam up to me and told me that he was surprised by the fact that though well past the obligatory retirement age, I was still working.

I held my tongue, but I thought, "Sure, I could retire, and then play cards everyday with you and Claude…" Certainly nothing wrong with a good poker game—I enjoy it from time to time, and these are nice guys to be with—but I should not be in the fix of having to look for pastimes. I talked to Henri then in terms of the things that were important to me about what I was doing, the needs they met for me. I am encouraged by Pablo Picasso's remark, "When they tell me I'm too old to do something, I attempt it immediately."[78]

While my choice to pursue working responsibilities may seem to contradict the theme of Ducket, it is my desire to spend my time doing what I value rather than being steered by others' expectations of "what I should be doing" or "what people my age should not be doing." As one of my own mentors once said to me, "Don't should on yourself. It makes a dirty, smelly mess of your life!"

So, don't git hit by shit that don't fit
The point of keeping your head down when requests for your time and energy are flying about at dangerously low levels, is not to duck everything, but to duck the things that don't fit for who you are and what you want to bring into being about you. Your Ducket list may also include things you are already engaged in, where stepping out or sidestepping might be the best for everyone. Later, when discussing Fucket, we will examine and sort through the superfluous activities and busyness that we impose on ourselves.

> *REFLECTION*
> *What socially imposed roles and goals are potholes in your daily commute toward who and what you want to be?*

Presence, not presents!

To lighten the burden of Chucket, use Ducket. If you can, say no in advance to gifts that will encumber your lifestyle. Steer your friends' love and generosity in the direction of giving to a good cause or showing up with something you really can use or share. Not always possible, as we are not always consulted about what we want, but when you can suggest, it keeps you from accumulating anything in your house that starts out as or will become a white elephant. When I throw myself a birthday party, the invitation I send always closes with, "Presence, not presents!"

REFLECTION
What kinds of things do I find myself doing just to be included?
How can I be more selective in meeting my inclusion needs?

 # A Docket of Seven Ducket Learnings

1. Ducket

As I write this, I am doing a lot of Yes work. I'm supporting the YES Scotland Campaign for an independent Scotland. I'm working with three clients using a process called Appreciative Inquiry, where we start with success and build toward the positive possibilities. And I'm leading my college class in imagining a successful 50th reunion. I like what my colleague Hans Harboe said: "I begin with Yes. Then I figure out how to make it work."

And yet, I acknowledge that the YES Campaign is saying no to the larger United Kingdom. I realize that even in Appreciative Inquiry, people sometimes need to look at the negatives in order to convert them to positives. I know that sometimes I need to begin with No.

Chucket is saying a complete No by taking something off my shelf. Shucket is keeping only the core of something on my shelf. And

Ducket is stopping that something from even reaching my shelf—or reaching my self.

Just last night, Rosie and I were sitting by the fire watching a TV program we both wanted to see. When it ended, Rosie flicked through the options for the next couple of hours and found two possibilities. Then we looked at each other and said No. Off with the TV and on with reading and conversation. Simple.

Tom Stoppard says that an exit is "an entrance somewhere else" so saying No to one thing allows me to say Yes to something else.

I learned a lot about the Ducket approach from Sonia Nevis. Sonia was one of my first mentors, working with me patiently and inspiringly during my five years of study at the Gestalt Institute of Cleveland. Here are three stories of what I learned from Sonia:

During my Gestalt training, I was struggling to finish one of the densely academic books about Gestalt theory. When I told Sonia about my difficulty, she said: "I finished that book before the author did." That wisdom has encouraged me to use Ducket on many books—and many other things—that are not worth finishing.

One day at the Gestalt Institute, when I was beginning to teach as well as to learn, Sonia found me in the staff room surrounded by books and desperately struggling with flipcharts. She asked what I was doing and I said I had to prepare a twenty-minute presentation on adult development. She said, "When I'm in that situation, I focus on speaking very slowly and saying very little." Although I'm still often tempted to say too much and say it too fast, Sonia's wisdom reminds me of the danger of that temptation—so I can Ducket.

And sometimes the temptation to say even a little is another chance to Ducket. In our third year of Gestalt training, we were working on interventions—when and how to say something that would help a person or a group move forward. Sonia gave us a challenge: "When you want to intervene, first think of three interventions before you say anything." At the end of the session, one of my colleagues complained about this process: "Sonia, this doesn't work; by the time I've come up with three interventions, the person and the group have already come up with something on their own!" Sonia just smiled sweetly. Ah, we realized, that is the point!

When I'm working with groups, I still use Sonia's wisdom. When I'm training others to work in groups, I pass on Sonia's wisdom— although I wait until I've thought of three other interventions first! Having wisdom is one thing. Letting others discover their own wisdom is even more powerful. That's the glory of Ducket.

2. Don't Ducket!

Even though a lot of things are worth ducking, there are certain things that I don't believe in ducking. It is now nearly two years since I wrote the above description of my first learning about Ducket and said "I am doing a lot of Yes work." I still am. In September 2014, we lost the referendum on independence for Scotland. But we moved Scotland from 30% for Yes to 45% for Yes. We have reached base camp and the summit is in sight. So, as the badge on my jacket says now, I'm **Still YES** and although the campaign for independence will now take more time and more work, this is such an important issue that I don't Ducket.

Another thing I don't believe in ducking is my responsibility to the people who will have to clean up after me, whether that's after I leave a hotel room or after I leave this life.

If I were still running a business, I would be creating a transition strategy for the business. Even as a consultant, I'm preparing a transition strategy. Although I am technically an independent consultant, I think of myself as an **inter**dependent consultant. So for years I've been working with other people who can take on my clients and my designs when I'm gone. That preparation has been extremely helpful in the past few years as I've been through five bouts of surgery. It's a relief both to my clients and to me that we know my colleagues can—and do—step in to keep things going.

Even on a personal level, I keep an eye on my transition strategy. I make sure that I update my will regularly and I update the other information in the "When I Die" file. And I continue to do the Chucket work on my other files. Many years ago I appointed George as my "literary executor" responsible for my written and digital heritage. He returned the "favor" immediately. As we grow older, we both want to make this responsibility easier for the survivor. It's another motivation to practice Chucket and Shucket on our collected outpourings—and not Ducket.

3. Duck Doing It Yourself

Some people are devoted to DIY: Do It Yourself. But I am devoted to DDIY: Don't Do It Yourself. If other people are really good at something, I would rather let them do it. This means it not only gets done right, this means it also contributes to society; I keep other people employed by hiring them to do what they have both the right tools and the right skills to do.

My lawyer father was the first one to tell me that if a lawyer chooses to act as his own lawyer, then that lawyer has a fool for a client. It applies to the rest of us just as clearly. One of my professional skills is coaching people in how to use energy and body movement to *rehearse* for an upcoming influencing situation. After my latest operation, I was trying to figure out how I could deliver this kind of coaching while still recovering from the surgery.

Then I went for a long walk with my friend Alan Raleigh, who has also been through this surgery. Fortunately, he has also been through several of my courses. When I mentioned my concern to him, he suggested that I *rehearse* doing some coaching to see how it went. I winced as I realized how often I tell others to rehearse. Then we both laughed. Even the coach needs coaching.

One challenge in being an independent consultant is finding people to give you the support and the challenge that you need to keep growing and developing—and keep finding work. Over the years, I've learned from hundreds of colleagues and thousands of students.

Some of them have become lifetime friends. Sonia once told a group of us that she had realized she needed a support network of twelve people—more felt crowded and fewer felt risky.

Years ago I realized that my own network size is eight or nine. In fact, I often refer to my special network of colleagues (four women and four men) as the Great Eight. When I include Rosie (although I often do her the kindness of not bothering her with my work), then I think of the group as the Fine Nine. I am particularly delighted that the Fine Nine were born in eight different countries on five different continents. With all those wonderfully different perspectives, they support me and they challenge me. They enable me to Duck doing it all myself, but they also keep me clear when it is my responsibility to do it rather than Ducket.

4. Flattery
Several years ago, a colleague in my professional organization phoned to tell me with great enthusiasm that I was the perfect person to develop an international group in our organization that would launch new programs and create fresh possibilities. I was reluctant—but flattered. And I liked the title: Steward. I accepted, but on condition that my friend Sushma Sharma in India be my co-steward. Together, Sushma and I created a sequence of new programs that we funded ourselves so that the organization could take them over and expand them.

I was proud of that but I was exhausted by the administrative tasks involved in the role. Speaking very kindly, administration is not my core competence. So, even though I liked some of the role and did accomplish some things, I encouraged another colleague to take over my role. By involving her, I accomplished stewardship in a different way: bringing a younger, female, newer member into an important position. And I put a sign on the wall in my study. "Flattery gets you in trouble."

Flattery that comes from others is difficult to resist. Flattery that comes from within me is even more difficult to resist. After all these years, I have a pretty good idea of what I know and what I do well. So when I see a situation where I can use my skills for the good, I flatter myself that I could help.

Robert Frost brilliantly describes this feeling in a wonderful title for a poem: *How Hard It Is To Keep From Being King When It's In You And It's In The Situation.*[79] I have pondered this dilemma again as I have resisted and at last accepted election to a local leadership role in the continuing campaign for independence.

Fortunately, I have learned a lot while serving as president of my college class for 45 years. I used to organize the class reunions every five years with just a couple of other people. For the 50th reunion, we have a team of 18 people working on it. One of the things I'm learning is to look for others who also see how hard it is to keep from being king. Then I invite them to work with me—so that we can help each other do the work that needs doing. And so that we can remind each other to notice the temptation to act like kings—and Ducket instead.

5. Paper
Incoming paper? Ducket! In the chapter on Chucket, I mentioned the wonderful David Sparks e-book called *Paperless.*[80] He says a lot about how to scan paper into digital format so that you can chuck the paper. Even more important, Sparks describes ways to avoid having that piece of paper on your desk in the first place.

First, stop other people from sending you paper. This takes some effort, but more and more organizations are happily shifting to electronic invoices and electronic messages.

Secondly, stop yourself from printing out that invoice or newsletter or email. I've been working on this one for the past few months and I'm getting much better at receiving an electronic invoice and simply saving it into the appropriate folder on my computer. That's a lot more sensible than when I was printing the invoice from my computer, scanning it, and then filing it back on my computer!

It is taking many months to get rid of the fifty-year backlog of accounts and other documents—but at least with Ducket I have stopped adding to the pile.

I've also discovered another advantage in asking people to shift from sending things by paper to sending email instead. When I get fed up with too much email, it is even easier to unsubscribe from the email—and Ducket completely!

Although I know that the true wisdom is to handle a piece of paper only once, I have great difficulty with that. I often leave the piece of paper on my desk to remind me to deal with it later. Hence the six-inch stack of paper next to me right now. The solution I began using some years ago was to put the paper into a project box—an open-sided box with a label on it for each client project or writing project or holiday. That at least reduces the places that I need to go looking for that piece of paper.

I am gradually moving toward scanning paper as it comes in so that I can search for things on the laptop rather than somewhere in my study. As I get better at ducking incoming paper, I hope that I'll also get better at ducking incoming electrons. I've begun by using smart folders in my email to gather less important stuff as it comes in, so I can look at it later. And I just went back to my email to unsubscribe from one organization. What if I did that every day?

As you get more serious about the Ducket approach, you may want to explore the idea of task management. This year I have started using the OmniFocus task manager software.[81] This software has already almost done away with the scattered lists of tasks on different pieces of paper.

It used to take me more time to find the list than it would take me to just do the task—if I could only remember what the task was. Now I'm entering the tasks into one system. I only have to enter them once—instead of again and again when I fill up a page but still haven't done all the tasks on it. And as I'm learning how to sort the tasks into groups, they only pop up when I need them. The entire OmniFocus process is helpfully explained by David Sparks[82] in a screencast during which he shows you how to set up and use the software.

6. Gifts

When Rosie and I got married, we were in our mid-fifties. We had both been married before. So we already had all those things that people give you when you get married. And since we were combining two households into one, we were actually giving things away. So we told our friends not to give us things, but instead to contribute to a charity. We raised several hundred pounds—and we ducked all those presents that we did not need.

As George has already said about his own celebrations, Rosie and I usually ask for presence rather than presents. And yet we know that some of our family and friends really like to give us presents. So when a birthday or other special time comes round, we ask for consumables. Cheese or jam tastes good—and never needs dusting.

With each other, we have shifted from giving things to giving experiences. Spending time together is more important than adding to the stuff we have too much of. This does require lots of Ducket when the catalogues, the TV, and the emails begin bombarding us with things to spend money on. So we shift to other parts of the web and look for places we would love to spend time together.

Except for some photos that we store online (and possibly a book to replace some other book on our shelves) we return from our days away with a slightly revised version of what Edgar Lee Masters said so delightfully about Fiddler Jones: A thousand memories and not a single thing to dust.[83]

7. Retreat

I'm imagining you reading this and expecting the seventh learning. That is a very powerful force: the force of expectation. And I want to meet your expectation—at least some of the time.

Yet I know that in order to learn something—and to realize that I've learned it—I sometimes need to go off by myself for a long walk or for an even longer time away from the world. Each year I look forward to my annual retreat: seven days of silence and solitude.

I first went on retreat more than forty years ago, when my lifetime friend Marianne Erdelyi said I was looking exhausted. "Why don't you just go away for a few days?" I did and I've done it every year since—except one.

That was the year 1976, when I was just a few months into a big contract as the local coordinator for an alternative university. I was doing great things with my students while simultaneously having great problems with my boss. So in April I decided I couldn't afford to duck out of my work for a week. And in June I got fired.

Looking back later, I was sure that if I had gone on retreat that year, I would have quit before I was fired. I would have had time to be away from the daily pressure so that I could recognize that my boss was never going to agree with me on how to work with students. But I didn't want to duck either the good requests from my students or the bad requests from my boss.

Eventually I remembered what I had learned while reading and writing military history for my master's degree. A wise general knows at least as much about how to retreat as about how to charge. In fact, an effective retreat is often what makes the charge possible. So I'll be off soon on my retreat—to recharge.

And when I return, I'll remember (as I do each year) that my regular annual long retreat is a reminder to take regular brief retreats all year. As the poet[84] says:

> *The world is too much with us; late and soon,*
> *Getting and spending, we lay waste our powers:*
> *Little we see in Nature that is ours;*
> *We have given our hearts away, a sordid boon!*

Sometimes I meet your expectations. Sometimes I don't. And sometimes I need a break before I meet your expectations. So I take a deep breath—and Ducket!

A sample Ducket List

 If you are wondering what your Ducket List might look like, here is the latest version of my own Ducket List to give you an example:

Flatpack furniture
Requests to join new organisations
Requests to join online groups
Invitations to sign up for new social media applications
Requests to like or comment on social media posts
Flattery from people who want me to do what I don't need to do
My own excuses for not doing things I do need to do

How to duck it

You've heard our own stories. Now it's your turn to Ducket.  Perhaps with a few more hints from us. So, when stuff is thrown at you, how do you duck it gracefully but effectively?

- Say thanks for the offer, and the trust it implies.
- Ask for the full details of what it may imply in terms of time, effort, skill, connections, or relationships.
- Show how its framework may not fit with your own priorities or indicate problems with timing.
- Accept some part of it, if that does fit your circumstances.
- Recommend someone whom you feel may do a better job of it than you.
- Offer to coach or mentor that person if you have something essential to offer.

Ducket checklist

If one or more of the following is the case, you might want to choose Ducket as your approach:

- ❑ It is not part of a serious commitment nor is it a moral obligation.
- ❑ It does not promote personal, familial, or social well being as I see it.
- ❑ It is same-old, same-old, and can't take me to an interesting place.
- ❑ It doesn't add learning or skills that I sense may be important to me.
- ❑ Doing it doesn't bring me in contact with those who are important to me or who might be interesting to work with or learn about.
- ❑ It is not in line with my beliefs and values.
- ❑ Its intensity and duration is oppressive.
- ❑ It will significantly disrupt my relationships with those with whom I live or who are important to me.
- ❑ It is not clearly defined and I am likely to be made a gofer for other's responsibilities or tasks.

REFLECTION
What is coming at me that I don't need to do? Am I ready to Ducket?

Under certain circumstances, urgent circumstances, desperate circumstances, profanity provides a relief denied even to prayer.

Mark Twain[85]

4: The Fucket List

Despite its title, this chapter is not about sex. When we began creating this life guide for ourselves and for other old guys, one of our ageing buddies thought that this chapter was about dispensing seminal fluids while the pump still worked and there were still some juices left in the reservoir. We're not excluding this possibility, but suggest that it fits on the Plucket List rather than here.

Instead, our focus here is on those times when, like Mark Twain, we feel so frustrated with something that we think or even say, "Oh fuck it!" Sometimes it's a justifiable reaction to stuff we've been doing forever that doesn't make sense any more, if it ever did. Sometimes it's about starting something that turns out to be too boring to pay off, or suddenly implies a lot more than we "signed up for" at the beginning. We accept that some things may turn out to have a steeper learning curve than we expected at the outset, but when a molehill starts to look like Everest, it may be time to utter those two magic words and move on.

What some folks think of as superfluous, others think of as essential—so it is important that the choices you make with Fucket are choices that help you lighten life all around and don't impinge on your promises to others. Of course such things may be negotiable, even after a long time, as you explore the mutual benefits of rethinking old habits.

Some have observed that as we age, there is a tendency in some of us older guys to "go to seed," to neglect our nutrition or our hygiene to the point of personal deterioration. That's not at all what we have in mind here. Quite the opposite. Rather, this is about enhancing the quality of life by preventing the superfluous from nibbling away at our precious hours and energies. It is time to look carefully. There are things about lifestyle, even food and cleanliness, that have been foisted on us by those who want to sell us something. Ageing might just give us the incentive to see whether our old habits are paying off or not. If not, the bird is always at hand to flip.

Everyday Fucket decisions

 As I reflect on my own story and continue to learn about myself, I can observe how my compulsions drift from one thing to another. I have betimes been a collector of everything from A (alligators) to Z (postage stamps from Zanzibar). "Stuff," as physical clutter is what we dealt with in Chucket and Shucket, but now we turn our full attention to debilitating habits and petty obsessions. Here are a few of the activities to which I have recently decided to say, "fuck it!"

Grocery accounting

Rarely an extravagant spender, I was still cowed most of my life by the so-called imperatives of money management and IRS tax reporting in my culture and so I kept every grocery receipt and entered each diligently into my Quicken accounting software. My finances, such as they are, are under control and relatively fixed, and I am sure that the IRS doesn't give a flying hoot whether I shop in the discount or the luxury aisle, whether I eat liverwurst or *foie gras*, glug jug wine at 2€ the liter or sip Chateau Latour at 150€ the bottle. So why track it? Fuck it! The same goes for the effort often involved in coupon shopping, though I was never a great devotee.

Reading obituaries

I stopped reading the closing pages of my several alumni newsletters some time ago, because they tend to be filled with death notices of people that I have not seen in over half a century and may not remember at all despite their then-and-now photos in the obits. As the eulogies are arriving regularly by email, linked to outpourings of "Facegook" from the same sources, it can be depressing even if they're folks I don't know. Certainly it hits home when somebody I really know takes up residence on the other side, but in these cases a friend or family member usually alerts me in short order.

Reading junk e-mail and punk snail mail and listening to that phone gunk

It occurred to me that I might use a piece of label paper to change the name of my computer's "delete" key to "Fucket." But even if I don't, I can still use that key *before* I read the obvious junk mail instead of afterwards! I've also been lobbying for a paper-recycling bin in the lobby where my apartment's mailboxes are located, a place to deposit punk snail mail and publicity stuffers without having to carry them upstairs to my wastebasket and then back down to the basement trash bin. Don't get me started about gunk phone calls, still legit here in France…I am not into *politesse*, but slick and deadly *finesse*.

Neatnikitis

I'm a neatnik. Been one all my life. "Every thing in its place and a place for everything." I was taught, "order is heaven's first law," before chaos theory became so popular that it is now a maxed-out plank of theoretical physics. Whether this trait is cultural or not, it certainly is a personal need. I can't get down to work without a clean workbench or desktop, wooden or pixilated. I pick up after others who leave things lying around. This probably won't leave until my next incarnation, but I need to manage it better in this one. More of feeling good about myself has to come from elsewhere than compulsive tidying.

Also, I really need to see when tidying up is a procrastination strategy for something else. There is a story about the novelist Ernest Hemingway meeting actress Marlene Dietrich at a party. In their conversation, she mentioned that she was going to write a book. Some months later, when they met again, Papa Hem asked, "Have you cleaned all your closets yet?" The Blue Angel blushed red with surprise and blurted out, "How did you know?"

Do I really have to put all the breakfast dishes away if I am going to need them for lunch? Fuck it!

Respect and deflect what you don't expect

Ducket was largely about avoiding inappropriate direct requests from others. You may need to Fucket in response to your own internalized demands about what you should be doing or in how you react to the demand of an unforeseen event. For example, when the Internet goes down, are you angry, bewildered, or delighted? The outrage of power outage could be offering you time for sage perspectives on what you are about and how you feel about it.

Some years ago in my small office in California, we were all green-faced from the reflected light of our computer terminals (remember the screens radiated green back then), when a truck took out a utility pole next to our building. After some moments of emptiness and annoyance, we rediscovered each other and reconnected richly, something that had been missing, though our open workplace had us seated only a few meters from each other.

Impromptu gathering gave us something no planned teambuilding event could. One world ended and we created a new one. The café across the street still had power, and this was when cafés served latte frappe without Wi-Fi. There were lots of work expectations on our heads, but much better to choose to Fucket for the time being instead of plunging into frantic attempts to change what we could not. Sometimes life makes an offer you can't refuse. An agile Fucket may help you flex and go with the flow.

Routine, Rituals, and Ruts

Habits allow us to not think about what we're doing . . . giving us the illusion of ease. When we are under the illusion of ease, not thinking about what we're doing, breathing the same old way, moving the same old way, thinking the same old way we check out of the present, out of happiness itself.

Alex Levin[86]

When deciding whether to say, "fuck it" to something I have been doing for a long time, it's important for me to take a close look in order to distinguish what is superfluous versus useful routine. Perhaps it's worth taking a few moments to distinguish among ruts, routines, and rituals. We make some activities routine, so that we don't have to think about them and they keep our everyday life rolling along rather smoothly. Medical evidence seems to show that there is great benefit in healthy routines to support us as we age; for example, a physical exercise routine that keeps us healthy.

Some routines become *rituals*, things we do that hold our lives together at a deeper level than brushing our teeth and watering the plants. We honor the rituals we practice that comfort us and become sacred to us, part of our identity. Take for example Pablo Casals, the Catalan musician and conductor who at age eighty still started each day by playing Bach on his piano.[87]

Rituals may be self-discovered, or they may come from a religious or philosophical tradition that I have inherited or subscribed to. These habits of the spirit keep me balanced and centered, and are my way of connecting myself to my deepest values and sources of inspiration, as well as to others who may practice them with me or as I do. They are often their own payoff, defying the question, "What's in it for me?"

So what is critical here is distinguishing those healthy routines and rituals from the ruts that we get into or have been in for a long time. Days seem shorter in wintertime and even shorter in the wintertime of our lives; hence we want to make the best of them and Fucket is an appropriate response to those behaviors that are not serving us physically, emotionally, or relationally.

Some routines and rituals can go out of date or become irrelevant over time, so it's good to raise the question about their ongoing benefits and whether I should modify them, or simply let go of them. Sometimes I only know their importance after I have dropped them for a while. There is no shame or blame in starting again.

As we said earlier about how to use this book, the seven ways in these chapters are closely related to each other. Not surprisingly, when we chuck out something, behavioral ruts connected to it head for the trash barrel as well. The same can be said for the changes of attitude or activity that follow on shucking or ducking something and, when we say Fucket to something, we may be left with a residue of material stuff that can now be packed up and sent on its way as well.

How I co-discovered the Fucket List

Although I've lived in Europe for nearly 35 years, I was born in the US. I'm a bit tired of the transatlantic flight by now, so I only return for the occasional reunion of family or friends. In 2012, I combined half a dozen reunions into one ten-day visit. While working with a team to prepare for our 50th college reunion and then while attending my 50th high school reunion, I heard lots of people talking about their bucket lists—all these things they wanted to do before they died.

I was puzzled by these conversations because for some time I'd been thinking in the opposite way. Since the WOW (Wiser Older Woman) I'm married to is a wee bit older than I am, we had already begun discussing things that we no longer needed to do. And my friend Johnny King had been sharing his delight that he did not need to do the things that he had thought for years that he *did* need to do.

So as I sat listening to yet another conversation about bucket lists, I realized (with the contradictory, polarity-alert, rhyme-fascinated brain that I have) that I was much more interested in the opposite of a Bucket List. And the opposite of a bucket list—in approach, in style, in language, and in rhyme—was obviously a Fucket List. I

The Fucket List   75

risked saying this to a few of my friends. First, they laughed. Then they took me seriously.

And George took me very seriously. Which has led to this book full of non-Bucket Lists. And most remarkably, it has also led to our realization that all these non-Bucket Lists are ways of clearing away what is not on your Bucket List so that you can get on with it.

The weird and wonderful Urban Dictionary website[88] encourages people to invent and define new words. According to that site, several other people have also come up with the idea of a Fucket List. Fortunately, we are not competing for a Nobel Prize so there is no need to prove who came first. We can just share the glory of the IgNoble Prize for thinking up such a great word.

Although we are offering you seven *ways* to live your life—from Chucket to Tucket—I do want to speak up for seven *lists* as well. In addition to making lists of things to do today, I also make ...ucket Lists. The Chucket, Shucket, Ducket, and Fucket lists remind me of what I want to clear from my life and the Plucket, Trucket, and Tucket lists remind me of what I want to focus on in my life.

After a frustrating hour this morning of struggling to screw together a new desk chair, I was tempted to add a Screwet list, but two other lists covered the ground already. On the Ducket List, I added *Flatpacks* and on the Fucket List, I added *Wasting my hands on tasks that others could do better,* which I need to remember because of the constant temptation to use my hands to twist or turn things. After 25 years of chronic pain in my hands and arms, I am learning to stop sooner.

So the Chucket List—with things like shredding old accounts—is a list of things to do that I can cross off when I've done them, while the Fucket List is a continuing reminder of things to *not* do!

When I turned 70 I knew that if my father were still alive, he would have reminded me that I was entering my eighth decade. In the language of the *King James Bible*, I became three score and ten. But that's no longer very old. And with Lincoln's words ringing in my ears from the recent film about him, perhaps I need to prepare for being four score and seven. Bruce Bigelow, my college roommate, now lives in Gettysburg; so I must ask him if he plans to still have a Gettysburg address when he is four score and seven. (If you don't like brilliant puns or bad jokes, please feel free to employ the Fucket approach and skip the rest of this chapter.)

The paradox of creating a Fucket List is that it helps me focus more time and energy on the remaining items on my Bucket List.

Seven Questions about your Bucket List

Before you get too upset with the idea of a Fucket List (or too delighted—most of the people we've shared this with seem to love the idea), let me reassure you that I do think it's fine if you also have a Bucket List. I just have seven (as usual!) challenging questions—for myself as well as for you—as I review the items I might find on my Bucket List.

1. Why haven't I done this already?
2. When is enough enough?
3. How much is enough?
4. What am I trying to prove?
5. Who am I trying to impress?
6. Who says I have to do this?
7. Who cares what other people think?

And here are my responses to those questions about what's on my Bucket List:

1. Why haven't I done this already?
For me, that has to do with two words that can describe the things on my to-do list in four ways. Some things are *urgent*, some things are *important*, some things are *both urgent and important*, and some things are *neither urgent nor important*.

I tend to do the urgent things (laundry or taxes) first and then the things that are urgent and important (responding to clients or sending out invoices). Eventually I get round to the important but not urgent things (like calling a friend or going for a walk). But it's the things that are neither urgent nor important (reading junk email or looking at comments on websites) that really slow me down and get in the way of doing the important things.

So it's that unimportant and non-urgent stuff that I need to keep on the Fucket List and off my doing list. For instance, the phone rang a minute ago. I ignored it so that I could keep writing this. As I did so, I remembered the wonderful story about an old guy who lived in the early days of telephones. One day he finally got a phone installed. That evening he was sitting on the porch with a visiting friend when the new phone started ringing. When the man made no move to answer the phone, his friend said, "Why aren't you answering your phone?" He said, "I had that thing installed for *my* convenience."

Another reason I may not have done this already is that I was waiting till I could afford it or until I had the time. That has to do with choices. Dick Bolles wrote a wonderful book called *The Three Boxes of Life*[89] in which he describes the choices we make about those three boxes: Learning, Working, and Playing.

Dick points out that for many of us the expected approach to life is to focus on Learning for 20 or 30 years, then focus on Working for 30 or 40 years, and then finally do some Playing for however many years are left. There are two problems with that approach—there may not be that many years left and you may not be able to do all the things you want to Play at.

So you have choices. You can balance out the three boxes every year, so that you do some Learning at a course, some Working to bring in the money, and some Playing on your annual holiday. Or, you can even balance the three boxes every week or every day. Then you don't have to wait till you can afford it or wonder why you've never got round to it.

2. When is enough enough? and 3. How much is enough?

"When I get older" is one answer to when enough is enough. With age, I may realize that I've got enough of some things. But the question of how much is enough is a tougher one. A researcher asked people across a range of incomes how much money they would need in order to feel secure. Whether people had a hundred in the bank, or a thousand, or a million, or ten million—the answer was always the same: twice as much as I have now.

One of the great moments of getting older—or getting wiser even before you get older—is when you start downsizing instead of upsizing. How many books are enough? Fewer than I had last year. How much travel is enough? Less than last year. And so on.

4. What am I trying to prove?
and
5. Who am I trying to impress?

It's tough being a guy. Our genes or our culture (or both!) get us into head-butting with other guys even when we don't need to do that. Sometimes when I'm working with a new group of colleagues, I just comment that the women may have to be patient for a few minutes while the guys do a bit of head-butting—and then we can get on with our real work.

I remember when that book came out with the line: "Real men don't eat quiche." I got fed up with hearing that, so I came up with my own line: "Real men don't read books about what they're supposed to eat." Which, as I think about it now, was just another head-butting response to a guy with a different opinion from mine.

6. Who says I have to do this?
and
7. Who cares what other people think?

The short answer to the first of these two questions is just to respond with the second question! Before the assumptions of I *have to* take over, I can consider whether I *choose to*. If I don't choose to, then it's time to Fucket.

To clarify the difference between *have to* and *choose to*, just make a quick list of ten things you *have to* do. (Pronounce *have to* as *hafta!*) Then challenge yourself (or have a friend challenge you) to explain why you must do each of those things.

There is an important distinction between *have to* things and *choose to* things. And it's not about the things themselves—it's about how you approach them.

Actually, you don't *have to* do anything. You may prefer to breathe, drink, eat, care for your children or parents, earn a living, give presents, etc. But you do not *have to* do any of those things. You can *choose to*—or not. Even if the result would be death or an unpleasant life, you could still choose that.

This is not just playing with words. I notice the difference in how I feel about the other person when I say that I *have to* read a story to my grandchild or I *have to* give my friend a present. The pressure of *have to* can lead to resentment and frustration with that other person—and when that other person notices the resentment then the relationship gets even worse.

I feel very different inside when I say I *choose to* read a story or I *get to* give a present. Then a burdensome task becomes a delight.

And I can choose to Fucket when I realize that I've been surrendering to someone else's (or even my own) expectation that I *have to* do something.

Now that I've answered those questions about a Bucket List, I can move on to my Fucket List. First, let me clarify again how we are distinguishing the various …ucket ways from each other. Chucket is about dumping stuff I don't need. Shucket is about getting rid of stuff that hides the core of what I need. Ducket is about dodging the demands that come from others. That allows us to think of Fucket as a way to get rid of demands that I make on myself—although some of them I may have originally picked up from others. Wherever it came from originally, it's now deep inside me, sapping my time and my energy. Time for a Fucket List.

So, here's my own current Fucket List. With luck, you might find some things for your own list. If not, then just say Fucket.

 ## My Fucket List: Seven things to leave behind while I get on with my life

1. Resentment
Looking back over my life, I can still get angry with the people who betrayed me, lied to me, used me, or ignored me. Some years ago, I woke up one morning feeling resentful toward a colleague who had wronged me—and I suddenly realized that he had probably awakened happily and gone on with his day without a thought for me at all.

So instead of my colleague suffering for his bad behavior, I was suffering twice: first from his behavior and secondly from my own resentment. Even I could figure out—eventually—that this didn't make sense. So, time to say Fucket.

Resentment can and does still hook me, but by keeping it on top of my Fucket List, I remind myself to keep letting it go. As with many things on these lists, I'm helped by remembering Charlie Seashore's great wisdom[90] about how we change our behavior. Charlie said he didn't think most of us could actually change our behavior completely. What we do instead is to realize how stupid or ineffective a particular behavior is.

At first, we may realize this several years later. As we become more aware of our behavior, we may realize the stupidity or the ineffectiveness within months or even days after we do it. Gradually, with lots of work, we can realize it within minutes or seconds. Eventually, we get good enough that we can sometimes catch ourselves just *before* we say it or do it.

So my resentment still pops up. But I recognize it a lot sooner and I move away from it a lot faster now. Sometimes, anyway. When it hangs on, I say to myself: This resentment is a waste of energy. Fucket.

2. Guilt

Looking back over my life, I can still feel guilty about the people whom I have betrayed, lied to, used, or ignored. In this case, when I wake up feeling guilty about what I did many years ago, then the focus is wrong again. I'm not the person to focus on; I need to focus on the other person.

When I focus on the other person, that gives me at least three options. I could ask forgiveness. And if I do that immediately, it may help. But expecting forgiveness is a second imposition on someone I have hurt already. And asking for forgiveness may raise the whole issue all over again, just when the other person has finally managed to get over it.

A second possibility is that I could provide some reparation—either directly to that person or to someone else. In the summer of 1964, I was filling out an application form to go to Mississippi with SNCC, the Student Nonviolent Coordinating Committee. When I got to the question about how many times I'd been in jail while protesting for civil rights, I got scared. I'd never been to jail and I didn't want to go to jail. So I didn't go to Mississippi.

I felt guilty about that decision—which is one reason that I later spent several years working in a project supporting race and sex desegregation in schools. And I continue that reparation in my diversity work with clients. Even if diversity is not on the agenda, I name racism or sexism or other isms when I see them in myself and in others.[91]

A third option is to do what people did at the Truth and Reconciliation Commission in South Africa. I can simply tell the truth and apologize—without expecting forgiveness.

Perhaps the strangest thing about feeling guilty about what I've done to someone else is that I'm assuming the other person is still feeling resentful. Maybe they've discovered, like me, how fruitless that is. In which case, we can both relax—say Fucket—and get on with our lives.

3. Anger

When I wrote the first draft of this section, I started with resentment and guilt—and I forgot about anger. That doesn't really surprise me. I'm still not comfortable with being angry or responding to the anger of others. That doesn't mean I don't get angry; it just means I don't do it very well.

I can get outraged by an unhelpful call-center person—and thus deprive myself of getting what I want. Several years ago when our Internet went down for several days, I got furious because each time I called there would be a new person who wanted to start over with the same questions. It took me days to realize that I was getting in my own way. I actually had to say Fucket to my own frustration and then make the next call calmly—and successfully.

I am slowly learning not to get angry at people who can only say no. Just two nights ago in a restaurant, when the waitress said our whole table had to order either from the set menu or the regular menu, I got angry and then I realized that she could only say no. So I calmed down and asked to speak to someone who could say yes. When the manager appeared, we got what we wanted.

My challenge with anger is to decide what is worth being angry about. Being angry at friends or family about small things just gets in the way of our being happy together. And being angry at cold-calling salespeople is a waste of time. I want to save my anger for the times that Reinhold Niebuhr referred to when he spoke of having "the courage to change the things that should be changed." [92] It's more important to be angry about what is happening to our planet's environment or to be angry about the increasing inequality between the few rich and the many poor.

As Bertolt Brecht says in *Mother Courage*, anyone can be angry; the question is: *How long are you going to stay angry?*[93] When it's worth staying angry, then I want to put my energy there.

When it's *not* worth being angry or staying angry, then it's time to say Fucket.

4. Curing

One of the great temptations in life is to believe that other people would be happier if they were more like me. I learned a major lesson about that many years ago when I was training a colleague to deliver a training course. One evening I was giving him feedback and he asked me when the positive feedback was going to begin. I said, "This **is** the positive feedback!"

That led to an interesting discussion and to my realization that what I thought of as positive feedback was telling him how he could be more like me. What could be more positive than that?! And that meant that negative feedback was obviously about how he was not yet like me.

Once I realised that the terms "positive" and "negative" were just confusing attempts to pretend that my subjective reactions were somehow objective, I developed two new terms for giving feedback. I now give **Keep feedback** and **Change feedback**.[94] "Keep doing this—if you want to influence me effectively." And then "Change doing this—if you want to influence me more effectively."

The key to this approach is that I am reporting on what works for me. The other person is free to use the feedback or not. And I am no longer trying to **cure** that other person. This point on the dangers of trying to cure other people[95] comes from David Keirsey, who writes about the different temperaments that people have. He describes that temptation to cure the other person—by making them more like myself. And he suggests we listen instead to the plea from the other person that he uses as his title: *Please Understand Me*.

Not surprisingly, I am much more aware of other people trying to cure me than I am of my attempts to cure them. When I sense that someone is trying to cure me, I'm getting better at saying Fucket (usually just to myself!) and walking away. The tougher challenge is to notice when I'm trying to cure someone else—and then to also say Fucket and walk away from that temptation.

As you read these learnings—and the other ideas in this book—remember that we are sharing stories of what works for us. We are not trying to cure you; instead, we are encouraging you to explore what might work for you. Try it out, take what works. For the rest, Fucket.

5. Access

I have too much access in my life. In 2006, Dan Saffer coined the term "topless meetings" to describe meetings where laptops were banned.[96] Now that I have my clock, my texts, my email, my radio, my travel tickets, my weather forecast, and my music all on something called my phone, it is increasingly difficult to go offline. But I do know where the off switch is!

Although I enjoy tracking my family's doings online, it is very tempting to read lots of other stuff that I'm not really interested in. So with social media and the web, I am working at just turning them off and saying Fucket to what I don't really need to know.

When I wrote about anger, I described my outrage at being disconnected from the net. After years of struggling with modems and cables and other complications both at home and in hotels, I now expect to have wireless access whenever and wherever I want.

Gradually, I have realized that the downside of my having access to the net is that the net then has access to me. I am learning—slowly—to decrease that access. Working on this book is much easier in the middle of the night (it's 03:15 at the moment) because no one is trying to reach me by phone or Skype. Except when someone forgets about time zones. Although I am tempted to check my email even at this hour, I know that I get more done if I just leave that app closed.

Working late at night, going for a daily walk of an hour or so, writing in my journal after breakfast are all ways that I say Fucket to access. Each of these ways is a small version of what I've been doing each year for more than forty years: going on retreat for a full week. I have, as you might guess by now, created seven learnings on retreat.[97] For me, a crucial part of a retreat is the combination of silence and solitude. So I turn off access to  the web and slow down to notice the natural world around me.

Going offline can happen in other ways. Several years ago, Ilya Sloutsky invited George and me to do a week-long workshop on a riverboat in Siberia. No internet or other distractions. Just plenty of time to enjoy the sunsets—like the one in this photo that Ilya took one evening. Sometimes paradise is just the absence of access.

Because I do like to have access to others most of the time, I understand how other people (family, friends, clients) expect to have access to me all the time. It's tough to take my own time, but I know that I need it. So every day for a few minutes and every year for a week, I say Fucket and go offline.

6. Fear

Fear is often a sensible reaction. When Rosie and I were blown off our feet by 100mph winds on a Scottish hillside, I was scared. When I flew into Darfur for work with the World Food Programme, I was scared. When I was diagnosed with cancer, I was scared.

On that windy hillside, we stayed off our feet and instead crawled along on all fours—using the heather roots to pull ourselves over the ridge and down the other side. When we got down a bit further and were approaching the risky river crossing that had seemed easy on the way up, I kept visualizing the sequence of stepping successfully from one rock to the next. And we both got safely across the river and down the hill.

I used a similar process in Darfur by keeping my focus on the work I was doing to inspire the people there—who kept inspiring me! And when I heard the cancer diagnosis, I cried and got a hug from Rosie; then I shifted my focus to images of keeping myself alive—and getting more hugs from Rosie.

In 1986, a few days after the Challenger disaster, I sent out one of my Learnings newsletters, entitling it *Here Be Dragons—and Dreams*.[98] Here is part of what I wrote:

> *These seven people died while doing exactly what they wanted to do. I think that explains why I feel inspired as well as shocked and saddened. Certainly it is dangerous to venture into the unknown. Centuries ago when explorers sailed into unknown oceans, they carried maps on which the mapmakers had written Here Be Dragons. James Lipton wrote an excellent essay on that theme some years ago in Newsweek and I have kept those three words above my desk ever since. His point was simply that wherever the dragons are is also where the challenges are. If I really want to live, to pursue my dreams, I must be prepared to go where the dragons are.*

So, the Fucket response to fear is not always to walk away from the fear. Sometimes the response is to say Fucket and walk *toward* the fear. In his essay, James Lipton[99] says:

> *I am speaking of the kind of risk-taking that seems to be involved in the conspicuous abandonment of safe physical, emotional and intellectual redoubts, in favor of new paths where dragons may lie in wait. I am*

sacrilegiously equating a state of fear with a state of grace, if the fear is evoked by testing treasured beliefs and established patterns—one's own, not someone else's.

So, I was also scared when I quit my first—and last—full-time job, in the middle of a recession. And I was scared ten years later when I moved across the Atlantic with only two weeks of work booked in Europe. But I faced the dragons—and found my dreams.

7. Expectations

Expectations may come from other people originally, but they get really dangerous when we accept them as our own. The psychological term[100] is introjection: swallowing something without chewing on it first!

My maternal grandfather was Walter Painter. My mother was one of four sisters. One never married, but my mother and the other two sisters produced a total of five more girls before I arrived. When I was born, I was the first boy in two generations. So I was named after my grandfather: Walter Painter Hopkins. I feel the honor and the responsibility of bearing both my mother's name and my father's name.

When I was eight years old, Grandpa Painter died. I was one of his pallbearers. After the funeral, one of my aunts said to me: "Walter, you are the man of the family now."

I swallowed that expectation. Completely. I never even questioned it until I was in my thirties. In my forties I considered buying the Painter home to keep it in the family, and in my fifties I crossed the Atlantic for reunions and for the funerals of all three of my aunts.

At family reunions, I was the master of ceremonies and I would introduce myself as the patriarch of a matriarchy—because although I was standing up front, I was always thoroughly briefed by at least one of my aunts and sometimes all of them plus my mother. I am more alert to my own tendency as a guy to be patronizing because of my own experience of being matronized.

Eventually, after many painful conversations, I accepted that I could still love my family of origin without taking responsibility for them. I let go of that responsibility and found myself much freer to focus on my family here in Scotland.

Expectations come from everywhere and if I don't dodge them with Ducket, I may need to use Fucket to get rid of them.

Of course, if I do chew on an expectation and decide that I like it, then it becomes part of me and I move on. Until, perhaps, another expectation challenges me. I got a watch for my birthday as a teenager and wore it for about ten years. When my first mentor, Dick Beyer, came back from a summer in California, I noticed that he wasn't wearing his watch. He said he'd stopped wearing one. I thought about it, said Fucket, and haven't worn a watch since.

Years later David Berlew, another mentor, wore a relaxed chamois shirt to a dinner where the rest of us were in jacket and tie. Gradually I too stopped wearing a tie, although I still wear a jacket sometimes. But most of the time now, I too wear a chamois shirt. Even my mother might support me now. She used to believe that I should wear a jacket and tie just to board an airplane. But she also had a consistent response when I would ask to do something because other people were doing it. "You are not other people."

One of the glories of ageing is finally realizing that I don't have to worry so much about other people. The title of one of the wonderful books about the physicist Richard Feynman is very clear: *What Do You Care What Other People Think?*[101]

My father gave me good advice on this point. When my college girlfriend broke up with me, he drove down to see me and to listen to me. A few days later I received a letter with these words—which I keep on the wall in my study:

There is some necessity for being, or learning to be, in some degree independent of what anyone thinks of you, even the person for whom you care most. You have to think so well of yourself that in the end you cannot continue to care in the same degree for a person who does not care for you. The paradox is that when you have learned this to a certain extent it sometimes works out that you are a better person and more cared for by the other person.[102]

I think of Feynman and I think of my father when I get too concerned about what other people might think of my clothes, my political beliefs, my emotional reactions, my work, me. As Fritz Perls said:

I do my thing, and you do your thing.
I am not in this world to live up to your expectations
And you are not in this world to live up to mine.
You are you and I am I,
And if by chance we find each other, it's beautiful.
If not, it can't be helped.[103]

Perls wrote that "Gestalt Prayer" in 1969, just as George and I were beginning to learn about the Gestalt approach that Perls and others developed. Those words appeared on lots of posters in the 70s, often (unfortunately) without those crucial last words: "If not, it can't be helped." In other words, Fucket.

A sample Fucket List

If you are still wondering what a Fucket List might look like, here are some more items as an example:

My belief that my accent gets in the way
Reading long lists of comments on social media
Risking pain in my hands by doing tasks that others can do
My belief that my background gets in the way of my foreground

"One great thing about growing old is that nothing is going to lead to anything. Everything is of the moment."

Joseph Campbell[104]

5: The Plucket List

Many of us may remember the taste of garden-fresh tomatoes or strawberries from the backyard patch. Whether our youth was urban or suburban or way out in the boonies, we are likely to recall the taste of fresh produce when it was actually in season.

Sweet corn, for example, is a delicacy that we two Ohio boys remember vividly. We were taught to pluck it, shuck it, and take no more than thirty minutes from garden plot to kitchen pot. Or, of an evening, just pluck it, dip it in water, wrap it in tinfoil, and nestle it briefly in campfire coals. It is disheartening to see three ears of already steamed sweet corn that has traveled all the way from Japan in the local supermarket at a price that would have bought dinner for both of us back then!

The fresh diet of our youth may have come from the corner grocer or from the "Victory Garden" that parents and grandparents nurtured in the backyard or on a plot down the road as their survival response to the Great Depression or as their patriotic contribution to the grim days of World War II. It wasn't just our youthful taste buds that gave the heightened flavors we remember. It came from the better taste of things plucked, shucked, and sucked in season. Urban guerrilla rooftop gardening is a movement currently taking shape and we oldsters can knowingly cheer, "More power to ya'!"

Marta goes shopping

As the Berlin wall came down and the Iron Curtain parted, I was

lucky to have in my California office a studious young intern, who came from Poland. Marta was enchanted with the size of the

Safeway store down the street. She was eager to learn about the intercultural work we were doing, and loved to share her native cuisine with the rest of us. Marta would come back from the store with the best (and priciest) produce, peaches from Chile, hothouse tomatoes, and other imported off-season items. Her thinking was that if it cost more, it had to be better—part of her sense of the USA as the "land of opportunity," despite the fact that our street was not "paved with gold."

Marta found it hard to believe that the tastiest items could in fact often be the least expensive because they were abundant and in season. The moral of this story is that, though we've all become a bit inured to the artificially "ripened" fruits and airlifted vegetables of every variety being available at any season, keeping our eyes wide open, we can find truly tasty bargains in season, not just at the grocery but at other places in our lives.

Seize the moment!
Ageing tends to remind me that, like ripe cherries hanging low on the tree, there are fruits, which the generosity of life may have been offering me for some time, things I have not noticed, resisted noticing, or simply said "no" to for some reason that maybe I can't quite recall—perhaps because I thought the pricier the better, or thought it too pricey without taking a closer look. Some may have been opportunities that I have passed by and will not come again.

I need to watch where I step; rotten apples are messy—but others are simply there for the asking, waiting for me to reach up or bend down, pluck, taste, share, and enjoy. *El interés tiene pies* as they say in Mexico, "What is interesting has feet," in other words, it can be fleeting—chase it down! Some of us may be well off, and price is not a consideration, while others of us may be struggling with the limitations of retirement income and look for a bargain wherever we can find it. In either case, it is the taste that matters, the enjoyment that counts, the opportunity that beckons, in what is readily available—often made more delicious by sharing.

Plucket asks you to examine why you may have ignored certain of life's offers. Plucket invites you to consider changing the rules of your game to take a second look. Now is the time. If not now, when? If not you, who? This may be good advice at any age, but especially at ours. The music group Incubus sings it well:

> *I've waited all my life*
> *If not now, when will I?*
> *Stand up and face the bright light*
> *Don't hide your eyes*
> *It's time.*[105]

Maybe you were taught to "strike while the iron is hot" and "the one who hesitates is lost," or maybe you were taught to "look before you leap" and "caution is the better part of valor." Both kinds of personal preference and ancestral sagacity are useful in the right context—and many of us heard both, or some variation of them—but somehow they may be delivered in such a way as to leave a lopsided preference in our life and work. Such habitual thinking may be depriving us of enjoyment or success that is neither costly nor hard to come by. Some of us may have been taught to pluck everything and find ourselves in need of Chucket and Shucket before we more selectively continue to pluck.

"Never pass up a bathroom."

George in Finland.

On the other hand there are everyday things that urge us to seize the moment if not *carpe diem,* the whole day. In the film *The Bucket List,* Edward Cole, the character played by Jack Nicholson, remarks, "Here's something to remember when you're older: never pass up a bathroom, never waste a hard-on, and never trust a fart."[106] For those of us with an expanding prostate or without one, the first piece of wisdom is useful Plucket advice. It is at least as old as

Napoleon's worthy adversary, the Duke of Wellington, who was supposed to have said, "The wise man pees when he can; the fool only when he must."[107] Walt reminds himself of this wisdom regularly by referring to a preventive pee before leaving the house as having a "Wellington."

Some of us were Depression or WWII babies who learned to look but not touch; that is, we may have been schooled in a kind of frugality that prized self-denial. Paradoxically, "what goes around comes around," and what we learned then may fit the new ecological age, punctuated by financial crises, that asks us to walk lightly on the earth.

Plucket is not about "having it all"— leave greed to the Gordon Geckos and the financial marketplace—but don't miss the invitation to satisfy yourself more fully with what is at hand and beckons you. Of course, we should at times ask ourselves "Why?" but perhaps we should habituate ourselves to "Why not?" as our leading question.

Plucket—is it a sin for men? Some of us were also schooled in the narratives of the Judeo-Christian Bible and recall that our journey of history, according to the Genesis tale, started with the Plucket behavior of a silly girl named Eve. Her curiosity about the taste of good and evil fruit from the orchard of Eden made wanderers of us all, ever in search of "the good old days." The hesitant, "don't touch" Adam in us should be ever reminded that his girlfriend's curiosity made us aware of our nakedness and so made her the Momma of all we come to be and to know.

Some fruits may turn out sour, but no pluck, no luck. The "good old days" are *now!* My current theological surmise is that the deity of Genesis is in fact a trickster who knows well that we can't resist forbidden fruit for very long. As Elie Wiesel so aptly put it, "God made man because He loves stories."[108]

Sometimes we hesitate to pluck it because of some higher purpose we feel committed to. This is honorable and praiseworthy—we want the fruit higher on the tree to ripen. The important thing is to be clear about our motives and how they help us climb the ladder to where the fruit is.

One of my mother's favorite anti-spending scripts was, "I'm saving for a rainy day." When she continued to say this to deny herself certain niceties when she was in her eighties, I remember once saying to her, "Hey Mom, look out the window, it's pouring!" Only later did I realize that I was her "rainy day." She wanted to make sure that I had something to inherit, though I was far from needy.

So, I need to remind myself not just to pluck for myself, but also to pluck for others, and encourage others to pluck from what I have to offer. Sri Ramakrishna suggests that *I* may also be the tree... "The tree laden with fruit always bends low. So if you wish to be great, be lowly and meek."[109]

It is difficult to judge others, but important to know myself. It's been said that there are two kinds of people in the world, those who eat the crust of the pie first and those who eat the filling first and the crust last. As astute as this observation is, it fails to tell us why. Some eat it first or save it for last because they find it the tastiest. Others eat it last or not at all because they don't fancy it or were well instructed as children "to clean your plate." Know thyself!

Plucking heartstrings

> *Remember when the music*
> *Came from wooden boxes strung with silver wire*
> *And as we sang the words, it would set our minds on fire*
> *For we believed in things, and so we'd sing*
> Harry Chapin[110]

Yes, I remember, and it reminds me that there are many forms of plucking. Back in those days, it was about dreams and folk music and no more war. At about that time, I became interested in playing a guitar, but was not very inspired by the instrument.

Then one day, walking home, my dad spotted a large black case sticking out of a dumpster. He plucked it and brought it home and I was suddenly the proud possessor of an antique plectrum banjo. That was my kind of instrument to pluck. Proof again, that "one man's junk can be another man's treasure." All you have to do is pluck it and then pluck its strings to your heart's content.

Some of us pluck strings; others of us pluck flowers. To each his own way of finding and making beauty in life. Each year on my birthday my friend Paul Westlake, who lives in Finland, sends me a large bouquet of flowers to decorate my celebration, reminding me of something that Walt said years ago, when housewarming his new flat in London: "Real men send flowers." It takes pluck to realize that.

Sadly, Harry Chapin fell victim to an accident just as, after much procrastination, I had finally decided to buy tickets to his live concert—a reminder that what I don't pluck may not be there when I pass by again. Harry still plucks his guitar in my iTunes, but it's not quite the same thing.

Try it; maybe you'll like it

Some years ago I felt a bit threatened when teambuilding went outdoors. Teams were taken to the woods to explore, help each 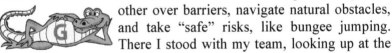 other over barriers, navigate natural obstacles, and take "safe" risks, like bungee jumping. There I stood with my team, looking up at the cable stretched between two massive California Redwoods.

When my turn came I was stuffed into a safety vest with string attached. I had to climb up the tree via some less-than-confidence-inspiring handholds and footholds. Then grasping a rope attached to one of the trees, walk across the cable from one tree to the other. I couldn't believe I was doing it but I did. Then back. Halfway on the return, I was instructed by my team leader to jump! Letting go of the rope, I consigned myself to nothingness until I was bouncing on the bungee cord near enough to terra firma to be brought in for a landing. I survived. Not only that, I wanted to do it again—this time with my eyes open! It took great restraint not to try to sneak into the queue of those nervously waiting to try.

Finally, it's hard to pluck anything when my hands are full or busy with something else. As you are reading this book you might have noticed that of our seven approaches for enriching your life, the first four are about emptying your hands, letting go, releasing your hold on what is no longer or may never have been in your best interests. They are ways of making time, space, and energy available for what really counts now and in your future, both what you need to get the most out of life and to give the most to it. So now it's time to Plucket.

 ## Seven Learnings about Plucking

1. Pluck it
To pluck is to "take hold of something and quickly remove it from its place."[111] I've been looking in the dictionary at how the word "pluck" is used by Shakespeare and others—and I've been learning some things. To pluck, I need to be bold and to take hold. It doesn't come to me; I have to reach for it. And grab hold of it. That corn in my grandfather's garden did not come to me; I had to go pluck it. Nikos Kazantzakis says, "I'm the kind who likes to grasp his dream like flesh."[112]

Our first four lists (Chucket, Shucket, Ducket, and Fucket) were about letting go of things so that we have our hands free to reach for other things. The transition between the Fucket List and the Plucket List is beautifully described by Benjamin Zander in a wonderful book called *The Art of Possibility*, which I encourage you to pluck immediately from your nearest bookshop or library.

As an orchestra conductor and a professor of music, Zander was asked by a young cellist for coaching in preparation for an orchestra audition. Zander worked hard to convince the young man to go beyond his basic professional skills so that he could "play from the heart" and share "the energy to take people beyond where they would normally go."

The young man was doubtful about this second way of playing, so he auditioned in his usual way for the associate principal chair in a regional orchestra—and did not get the job. Then, as he told Zander later, the young man was so angry, that he said, "Fuck it, I'm going to Madrid to play the audition for the *principal* cellist in the orchestra there." This time he played in the second way. And he got the job—at twice the salary.

Benjamin Zander called this approach BTFI (Beyond The Fuck It)[113] "which fast became part of the folklore of all my classes, and showed up in the students as a spiritedness in going beyond where before they might have stopped."

So when I say Fucket to something that has been getting in my way or slowing me down, I am now free to see something new and wonderful—and Plucket!

2. Pluck now

Not only can I pluck *now*, I can also pluck *the now*—the present moment. As someone who loves both history and science fiction, I find it easy to drift into the past or the future—thus missing the present. What I began learning in my years of training at the Gestalt Institute of Cleveland was to focus on the here and now instead of the there and then. That was forty years ago and I sometimes think it will take me another forty years to learn how to do it! Notice how easily I have just slipped into the past and the future while supposedly talking about the present!

Just now, I choose to pluck *the now*. The first thing that happens is that my shoulders drop an inch. Now I look out the window and notice a patch of blue sky above the fast-moving grey clouds. Clusters of colorful birds surround the feeder outside my window.

The willow tree is budding and the leaves of the first daffodils are peeking up in the garden. As the great French artist Henri Matisse says, "There are flowers everywhere—for those who bother to look."[114]

Now I come back from plucking *the now* and remind myself also to pluck *now*, lest I find myself asking with Dr. Seuss, "How did it get so late so soon?"[115] When I lived in Ohio as a boy, not only did I have to take hold of the corn, I had to do it quickly before the raccoons got it first. Now I live in Scotland and the changing weather here also teaches me to pluck now. If the sun is shining or if at least it is not raining, then it is time to walk now. And on the walk, I often pluck the now from the world around me—or from the world within me—and create a haiku.

> *When clouds are coming*
> *in behind the sun then the*
> *time to walk is now.*

In fact, the rain has now stopped, so I'm off for a walk.

3. Pluck again
It was raining by the time I got out the door. So that plucking didn't work. I need to move more quickly next time. And rather than getting myself stuck in the past by blaming myself for missing a past chance, I need to remember what the Canadian hockey star Wayne Gretzky says about plucking pucks: "I skate to where the puck is going to be, not where it has been."[116]

When I miss a chance the first time, I'm tempted to give up. But Gretzky comes right back with more wisdom for puck plucking and other kinds of plucking: "You miss 100% of the shots you don't take."[117]

I love the onomatopoeic sound of puck plucking! Grab now while you can—and grab again if you miss the first or second time. If you want to let off a bit of angry steam, then you can always use Benjamin Zander's BTFI and move from Fucket right on to Plucket.

4. Pluck often

I have an app on my computer that reminds me every 40 minutes to take a ten-minute break, get up, move around, and refresh body and mind. Little breaks from what I am doing often cause a switch in awareness that leads me to pluck other things out of the air. I first started doing these breaks back in 1990 after I developed RSI (Repetitive Strain Injury). Although I got RSI from too much computer work, the first people to be diagnosed with RSI were Australian chicken pluckers, people cleaning the feathers off chickens. Some plucking can be dangerous!

So it's worth switching my attention from one task to another and discovering what else I might learn. If I don't look up, I might miss something. I might get stuck thinking about *why* things are as they are—and miss the chance to wonder *why not* make things different. George mentioned the ancient dilemma we have inherited from Adam: Don't touch the forbidden fruit—or go ahead and pluck it.

In his play *Back to Methuselah*, Bernard Shaw sets the first scene in the Garden of Eden and gives this wonderful line to the Serpent as he tempts Eve:

> *You see things; and you say "Why?"*
> *But I dream things that never were; and I say "Why not?"*[118]

Saying "Why not?" allows me to imagine different possibilities and to learn new things. I first heard about the Duke of Wellington's wisdom from Peter Honey at a professional conference back in the 1980s. Peter transformed it into a way of encouraging voluntary learning instead of compulsory learning: "Wise folk learn when they can, fools learn when they must."[119]

So I aim to learn something every day—as my father did. I vividly remember the day when my father opened the top drawer of his desk to show me how his small box of pens no longer slid back into the drawer when he pulled it open. He had recently discovered that he could stick Velcro strips to the bottom of the drawer and to the bottom of the box. He grinned with delight at what he had learned. He was 82 years old.

5. Pluck low

Low-hanging fruit is easy to pluck. Just because it is easy need not stop me from plucking it. We all have different preferences: some go for the easy pickings and others (like me) make it tougher on themselves. Paradoxically, my challenge is to pluck the easy stuff.

Some time ago, I sent my brother Giles (who still plays basketball once a week) a video of basketball players taking long shots. He responded:

> *I always remember you like the long shot.[120] I always think of you when I talk about the research on motivation where they do the experiment of putting a wastebasket in one corner of the room and then have people stand in the opposite diagonal corner with three bean bags. They are told that they can stand anywhere between the corner and right next to the wastebasket and try to throw as many beanbags in to the basket as they can. Some people stand as far back as they can get and some people stand right next to the basket and others in between.*

> *The research shows that people who stand right next to it are more motivated by power (win the game), people who stand in the middle are more motivated by achievement (set a goal at the edge of their competence), and people who stand at the farthest point more motivated by affiliation (friendship, cooperation—perform for a positive impact on others—they want to both inspire and be appreciated for the long shot). I guess I am a bit that way too as I am known by my basketball buddies for playing the point guard who distributes the ball where*

others can achieve and occasionally taking the long three pointer for the game winner.

Each of us has a preference, but I don't have to limit myself to my preference. For me, taking the short or even the medium shot seems too easy. But if the shot is there, if the low-hanging fruit is right in front of me, then it's wise to pluck low.

6. Pluck long

This suits me much better. I like to reach. As Nikos Kazantzakis says in *Report to Greco*: "Reach what you cannot."[121] I love the long shot in basketball and even though I no longer play basketball as my brother does, I still watch videos of other people making half-court or full-court shots. I spent twenty minutes doing just that last night. When I was a kid, I would shoot from mid-court and make maybe one out of ten—but how delightful that one success is.

When picking cherries for my grandparents at the farm, I would reach high up beyond the top of the ladder to get those last few cherries. Back then I often celebrated by eating the cherries before they hit the bucket. Now I celebrate by eating cherries with equal delight before I kick the bucket.

Just now I am putting my time, my money, and my energy into two long shots that may bear fruit in 2016. I'm working with hundreds of classmates to raise a record-breaking class gift from a record-breaking percentage of participation for our 50th college reunion. And I'm working with thousands of people in Scotland on the YES campaign for Scottish independence. As I revise this paragraph in 2015—that second long shot did not go in. But we still have the ball and we are still aiming for another long shot in a few years.

When I quit my last full-time job more than forty years ago (in a recession), I took a long shot that I could survive as an independent consultant. Why not? There have been a lot of missed shots since then, but I keep taking the ball again—and shooting again. And some of those long shots do go in!

7. Pluck up

One way to use *pluck* as a verb is to say *pluck up*, as in deciding to pluck up courage. And even though we've been using *pluck* as a verb, *pluck* is also a noun, adjective, and adverb when it refers to courage, spirit, bravery, or in other words: **guts**. As many people have reminded me over the years, old age is not for wimps. In the past nine years, I've had five operations—including the removal of a burst appendix and the radical prostatectomy for prostate cancer. I've reached the stage that my friend Ed Mayhew describes as high maintenance for high mileage.

It does take pluck to "keep on keeping on," as Roy Fairfield[122] says. Roy was my doctoral professor 40 years ago and he is now thriving in his nineties. He has avoided Re-TIRE-ment by choosing to call it Re-FIRE-ment! Roy is the oldest person to read this book in draft—and he responded faster than anyone else. He ended his note with his usual farewell: "Keep on keeping on!" Roy is pure pluck and he plucks life pluckily. He inspires me to do the same.

James Graham, the first Marquis of Montrose was another remarkably plucky man—as I learned from researching his life for more than two years. In the mid-seventeenth century, Montrose fought a series of military and political campaigns while also writing prose and poetry.

The following stanza from Montrose's greatest poem [123] is a description of his own life—and a challenge to the rest of us:

> *He either fears his fate too much*
> *Or his deserts are small*
> *That dares not put it to the touch*
> *To win or lose it all*

Montrose has had a major impact on my life. He inspired me to come to Scotland as a graduate student and his words have challenged and inspired me whenever I was fearing my fate and needing encouragement to pluck it! Other courageous people also inspire me. In my book on influencing skills, I told three stories about people who influenced others with directness and courage. I'd like to share these stories again as true stories of people who influenced pluckily.[124]

In the first story, a man had been trying to connect with a woman for several months but he had given up. A friend encouraged him to risk one more call. He made the call and **pluckily** said to the woman that he wanted to be with her. They are now happily married.

In the second story, a woman discovered that a man was thinking of marrying someone else and **pluckily** said to him, "I always thought if you married anyone, you would marry me!" They have been happily married for decades.

And in the third story, a wise and wonderful woman told me lovingly and **pluckily** that if I wanted to live with her then I would have to marry her. Wisely, I did.

There is also a fourth story that connects directly with Montrose. When I was doing my research on Montrose back in 1968, I went to the door of a farmhouse in the far north of Scotland and asked the man who answered the door: "What can you tell me about the battle that took place in your back garden?" He said, "I didn't know there was a battle there!"

That got us to talking, and David Alexander became a dear friend for the next 42 years as we kept on talking—about Montrose's last battle there at Carbisdale and about many other things.

When I spoke at David's funeral, I told the story of how he struggled to work up courage to ask Kate to marry him. He told me that he often felt the spirit of Montrose walking those hills. And this time he heard the words of Montrose encouraging him to go for it. He did, and the two of them lived together lovingly for many years.

I repeat those words so often to myself that I'm going to repeat them to you now:

He either fears his fate too much
Or his deserts are small
That dares not put it to the touch
To win or lose it all.

A sample Plucket List

If you are wondering what your Plucket List might look like, here is the latest version of my own Plucket List to give you an example:

More days out with Rosie
More time campaigning for an independent Scotland
More time working with the World Food Programme
More time connecting, creating, and contributing to our 50th *reunion at Wooster*

Instant cybergratification

It is so easy to digitize life today. For example, I can Google information that I am looking for quicker than I can walk across the room to where I know it is stored in a file or book. When I was in college, I remember having a notebook into which I put questions I wanted to answer and topics I wanted to research. Then every Tuesday and Friday afternoon I would hike across campus toward the arms of the "Touchdown Jesus" monumental mural on the face of the Notre Dame library. I'd pull drawers from the card catalog and poke around the stacks for the right shelf and the right book and the right page on which my answers might be hidden.

Today I can answer most questions better and certainly quicker without budging from my chair. New technology has me learning a dozen times more in one day than I learned back then in a week or two. Now when it comes to knowledge, I can pluck it instantly. Should I shout "Yahoo!" in triumph as I Google on?

Likewise, when I first lived abroad in Germany in the late 1970's, an exchange of letters took at least two weeks and a twenty-minute international phone call could cost $90. Now I have got back friends from every age of my life, from grade school to those I met on a trip last week. Whatever corner of the world I find myself in, it's for free or next to nothing on Skype or Viber or FaceTime, assuming of course that both I and the person I am calling are out of bed in our respective time zones. Time has often taken friends from us, but the times allow us to enjoy old and new connections. Fresh ripened fruit, new opportunity is here. Pluck it!

That is certainly the up side. Without complaining, or taking either an old fogey or Luddite stance, it is worthwhile to ask what I may be sacrificing in context and connection from the time of my non-digital existence. Well, digital can give me more time and space for other things I enjoy. Having practiced Chucket on my bookshelf, I'm left with the delicious poets that I savor over and over again and the fresh arrivals I am anxious to explore. Okay, maybe more of these will vanish into my Kindle, where they are even easier to pick up whenever and wherever I want, though I still enjoy the pleasure of reading the spine of an old favorite, plucking it from the shelf, and cradling it in my hands. Pluck where you will!

A recent cartoon shows a person, laptop open, asking the question, "How long is it polite to wait before asking the folks you are visiting for their Wi-Fi password?" In many cases it is no longer necessary to entertain guests and wonder just what to do with them—they entertain themselves on your Internet connection! Let's learn to pluck the best of it and enjoy the rest of it.

Pluck it and Share it!

Much of our contemporary Western culture fails to esteem old age and too easily denies the relevance of what you and I have learned and can do. Though some youngsters may not want to hear my stories, quite often my age and sometimes my status gives me the opportunity to see and pluck things that others can't see or reach.

Plucking and careful sharing not only reconnects me with the other but helps me bridge the generations. One does not have to be rich or mobile or even have a social network on one's mobile to be able to pluck and share the riches.

Plucket can replenish our losses

Plucket is not just about enjoying ready satisfactions and satisfying my taste buds or my aesthetic tastes. More importantly, it speaks to 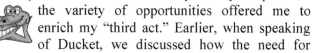 the variety of opportunities offered me to enrich my "third act." Earlier, when speaking of Ducket, we discussed how the need for inclusion could in fact betray our best interests.

Let's face it, however, the plot of the "third act" often involves disappearances, loss of job, community, family and friends, loss of partners, moving to retirement homes or communities, reduced mobility and resources, all of which may make us hesitate to reach out to others and ask whether we should just bid adieu or stretch out our hands in new directions.

Some of us may have leapt joyfully into retirement. Others of us have been hoaxed or coaxed into early retirement by the "reorganization" of organizations that no longer needed us or that wanted to pay someone less. It is important to recognize what we can chuck and shuck from our occupational past. As well as see how the spaces created by loss can be filled with satisfaction.

Some of us have had very repetitive jobs, others more variety. We may have had to work very hard at creating pride in performance and pleasure in motion. Best of course if we have been doing what we love, but many of us of also learn to love what we do. In either case, the now empty hours can either threaten us or beckon us. Our aimlessness or neediness can burden our partners and our families and distance our friends.

In my work I have discovered *Flow*, those brilliant moments of performance, so well described by Mihaly Csikszentmihalyi in his book by that name.[125] These are moments where time and effort seem to disappear and I operate in the sheer joy of now. This happiness does not have to disappear with retirement or disability because it lives in my heart and not just in my hands. Opening my eyes to what is right for plucking can lead me to use what I know, as well as develop latent skills and loves.

When it comes to relationships, it seems that the risks are mounting against us. Given our personality, are we likely to fall victim either to lonely introversion or superficial extraversion? Many of us live in an ageing world where the average age of the population is increasing steadily. Others of us live in "young societies" where the young vastly outnumber the aged and those like us may be harder to find and connect with. We may feel overburdened as one close to us passes into the need for constant care, raising our fear of heading in that same direction. We struggle to know what to do.

In his brilliant expositions of love, French philosopher Yann Dall'Aglio[126] points out that it is the reciprocity of desire that makes our love for each other work. And when love does not work, it makes our connection painful and our loss, paradoxically, can be more painful as it represents loss that has been going on often for a long time. When I lose an intimate by either separation or death, that emptiness requires real grief and then replenishment. The longer we have been connected to each other, the harder it is to do and the riskier it seems. There is no easy substitute.

What about the question of adding new friends and keeping old ones? How much do I need to know about others, their history, and the context I met them in and know them in? Do I want to make new friends? Expand my horizons and connections and support?

Or do I prefer to stick with old friends, the kind who know about past wives and past lives without my having to explain all that again. If I want to keep old friends, how do I maintain connections with them so that we don't drift away from each other?

Having a Plucket attitude is essential. Helen Keller was the first deaf blind person to win a college degree and went on to become an influential writer and activist. She reminds us that:

> *Avoiding danger is no safer in the long run than outright exposure. Life is either a daring adventure, or nothing.*[127]

Sometimes Plucket makes me feel a little bit like a naughty child plundering the neighbor's apple tree. But mostly it is about caring and being cared for. A year and a half ago, I was attending a friend's wedding in another country and, having exhausted my ballroom steps, was sitting on the sidelines enjoying the folk dancing when a young woman, a stranger, whom I had not met before this day, approached me, sat alongside me, placed her head on my shoulder and began to sob.

Not knowing what she was experiencing, I placed my arm around her to let her know it was okay. Later she began to tell her story: recent loss of a lover, the death of a father and, most of all, self-blame for all that had been happening. I wanted to offer continuing support, and was wondering how. I was only a visitor and leaving the next day.

I decided to do my best, to offer what I could at a distance. This amounted to writing her a haiku poem each day over the next months. Our exchange gave each other purpose and focus. We are still in touch.

> *The hurt seems so great.*
> *Sadly, I only send words.*
> *Want to give you more…*

> *You create beauty.*
> *How you look at what you see*
> *tells you what it is.*

We urge you to reflect and go on lovingly plucking. We leave you with the advice of Helen Hayes, a US actress whose career spanned almost 80 years:

The truth [is] that there is only one terminal dignity— love. The story of a love is not important—what is important is that one is capable of love. It is perhaps the only glimpse we are permitted of eternity.[128]

If I should not be learning now, when should I be?

Lacydes of Cyrene[129]

6: The Trucket List

Dictionaries define "Keep on truckin'..." as to persist—whatever the circumstances or setbacks, to keep trying or striving, or simply to continue putting one foot in front of the other. Many of us were hip when Robert Crumb created his famous one-page comic in *Zap Comics* in 1968, showing his characters stretching their huge feet forward in long strides as they kept on truckin' across the land.[130]

The phrase had antecedents. "You're doing a great job, keep on trucking" was a phrase of encouragement urging one to stay focused on a particular job or in general. The phrase is supposed to have originated in the marathon dance competitions of the 1930s in the USA, where the contestants clung to each other and kept on moving throughout the night (like long-haul trucks), even sleeping on their feet, but moving, moving. The saying was then adopted by jazz musicians, who said *Keep on truckin'* to encourage each other.

What Lenny Kravitz sang about a love affair, "it ain't over 'til it's over,"[131] can be the theme song of your continuing love affair with life, with the people and the causes that are important to you as you focus on what needs doing—in your own life and in the world.

And if you get discouraged, remember the situation that Yogi Berra was in when he first came up with the line: "It ain't over 'til it's over!"[132] Yogi says: "That was my answer to a reporter when I was managing the New York Mets in July 1973. We were about nine games out of first place. We went on to win the division."

This raises a few questions. Where should your persistence be taking you? What tune are you dancing to? What dreams are you continuing to make real?

Let's look at ways we can Trucket on three levels: body, spirit, and community. We believe that you can't have one without the others; they go hand in hand, each supporting the other. Here are some stories about that from Walt the Musician and George the Hippie.

The Musician

Sometimes we do our music in the classical style—with a conductor leading us through specific notes. When I sang with the Cleveland

Orchestra Chorus, our conductor Bob Page expected us to be as good as the great orchestra we were singing with. He once told us to come in on the second half of the third beat. Bob expected that kind of precision. A few hundred yards from Severance Hall, in a Cleveland restaurant called That Place on Bellflower, my colleague Frank Barrett was playing jazz piano with equal precision—and coming in on whichever beat felt right at the moment.[133]

One way to Trucket is to play your own jazz. Once when we were dancing, my wife said to me kindly that I danced to my own rhythm! She was echoing Thoreau's equally encouraging wisdom:

> *If a man does not keep pace with his companions, perhaps it is because he hears a different drummer. Let him step to the music which he hears, however measured or far away.[134]*

In the field of Organization Development and the field of Individual Development, we often speak about the Use of Self as Instrument.[135] This means that in working with other people, we pay careful attention to our own thoughts, feelings, and reactions. For instance, if I'm feeling sleepy that could simply mean that I didn't get enough sleep last night. Or it could mean that I'm bored by what's going on—and perhaps other people are also bored. So I could check that out by looking at others or even by taking the risk of asking others.

This does require great sensitivity! Imagine yourself being, even momentarily, as sensitive as GAIA, the European Space Agency's newest space telescope—able to sense distant stars while simultaneously maintaining your precise position between the earth and the sun.

Even if you are not, as George and I often are, working as a consultant with a group or an organization, you still have a critically important client: yourself. Even at those times when you do not need to be highly attentive to friends, to family, to the people you live with, you still need to be sensitive to yourself.

If you are a musician, when you pause in performing, your first task is to care for your instrument. The same is true for all of us. That means both taking the time to pause from performing and then taking the time to keep ourselves in tune.

This gets more complicated as we get older. I still remember the series of charts in a magazine that I read when I was twenty years old. Each chart demonstrated the peak and then the decline of various bodily systems, such as digestive, respiratory, cardiovascular, muscular, and so on. Every one of those charts showed declines beginning in the mid-twenties. And in the last fifty years, I have had numerous confirmations of the accuracy of those charts!

Fortunately, I have managed to keep myself in tune for much of the time by taking care of myself as an instrument of body, spirit, and relationship. Here is George with some specific suggestions for how to do that.

The Hippie

Sure, age inevitably brings wear and tear on the older bod, no denying it, but the trick is both managing it and integrating it.

An example. After 40 years I am a "hippie" once again—I have two prosthetic titanium hips. Although they require some cautions, I largely forget about them because they work so much more smoothly than the old arthritic ones did. They enable me to go where I will with a bike rather than a gas-guzzler, and I can swim a good distance to harvest mussels off the rocks in the bay. In fact, I am usually conscious of my metal hips only at the airport security check, where they never fail to set off all the alarms and earn me a free massage. I get to tease the inspector by asking for more pats around the shoulders and emitting a few oohs and ahs as different spots are examined.

In addition (don't tell anybody), as I so dislike the endless security procedures, I have another fun social protest strategy. If they ask me to take off my suspenders for the frisk as they often do, I do so obediently, but let out my breath, flattening my not-too-flat belly. This encourages my pants to drop down to my ankles, advertising my fresh pair of Hanes jockey shorts to the frustration of the inspectors and the hilarity of fellow passengers!

Mind management and ageing

So, how do we "keep on truckin'?" We often live in cultural surroundings where age is not valued in the work place or in society. The aged are often not very interesting to pay attention to. We need to reframe that for our own well-being and to empower ourselves to continue to contribute what we can to our world.

My mental tricks

Recently I was turned down for a university lectureship with the rationale that, though I was the most qualified candidate, I was over the legal age for employment. Go figure! Disappointed I most certainly was, so it was a concrete moment in which I needed to pull out something from my "Keep on truckin'" toolbox... Hmmm. What did I have?

A tee shirt. For my birthday several years ago, while coaching in Mannheim, Germany, I found and bought a tee shirt that reads: "Old-timer. Driven for over 70 years, a few scratches, but no rust, tip-top condition."[136] It highlights for me the need to both appreciate the years and honor where I am in life. A well broken-in vehicle can be a better buy than a balky new one. This frequently suggests the need to conquer both my own fears of ageing and irrelevance that are so often fueled by popular culture.

So affirmations even as simple as this tee shirt are not just humorous but something visible and tangible as well as relevant to morale building. I don't need to pretend to be younger again, but I do need to affirm my value, especially when it is called into question. More about this when we talk about Tucket.

Secondly, I speak French French (as distinct from Swiss French or Belgian French). Living in France I have created my own strategy for speaking of myself when it seems that I am relegated to more retirement than I actually feel and live. It's a language trick that takes advantage of the difference in how the years are counted in different francophone countries.

I tell people that I am lucky to live in France, because here I am in my sixties, sixty-seventeen *(soixante-dix-sept)* in French French, while in Switzerland or Belgium I would be seventy-seven *(septante-sept)*. Pushing it further, I say that in three years I will be back in my twenties again, at four twenties *(quatre-vingts),* rather than eighty *(huitante)* as I might be measured across those same national borders. Sure, it's a spoof that brings a laugh from my listeners, but also brings them to accept, acknowledge, and sometimes even remark about my current level of pizzazz and my determination to meet my needs at this moment in my life.

While we were working on this project, Walt linked me to a presentation by Jane Fonda, who is exactly my age (we were born three weeks apart) and whose energy and commitment to health and healthy society I much respect. I actually engaged with Jane in the planning of a Viet Nam anti-war demonstration in my town. Now she speaks to what our age has to offer ourselves and others—*a Third Act*—an upward potential for the human spirit and a new sense of well-being, whatever our aches and pains.[137]

Also, while we have been writing this, the French language has gifted us with a new label for ourselves. The newly approved word is *plénior*, a refinement of *senior*, putting the emphasis on the plenitude, the fullness of life to be found in our third act rather than on the accumulation of years of wear and tear. In this society it recognizes the older person, like Jane Fonda, who is thriving intellectually, emotionally, and materially, well enough to be enjoying life. *Merci!*

Age and social engagement

So, Jane Fonda provides me with a model bridge between health and social action, providing successful exercise programs and exercising political influence via protest.

You may remember Dr. Benjamin Spock either as the author of a best-selling book on baby and childcare or as a peace activist or both. When we recall the Viet Nam protests, he is always there. It is worthy of note that he "kept on truckin'" for peace and human rights until his death at age 94. An Olympic medalist rower, he kept on truckin' by an active and energetic, socially concerned life.

As the single child in my family, I enjoyed a nursery jingle whose words mingle the sweet effort of navigating life and tingle with the warning of danger to be managed:

> *Row, row, row your boat*
> *Gently down the stream.*
> *Merrily, merrily, merrily, merrily,*
> *Life is but a dream.*
>
> *Row, row, row your boat*
> *Gently down the stream.*
> *If you see a crocodile*
> *Don't forget to scream.*

A good life, as our coxswain Walt reminds us, implies steadily rowing in the direction of our dreams, especially our serious ones.

When a nasty croc shows up, it's time to take notice, warn the world, and take action. When we think of the causes that are important to us, it is important to include the kind of activity that keeps us healthy and supports us whatever our activity or activism.

For a game that I created[138] to share my commitment to *Cultural Competence*—learning to deal respectfully and creatively with human differences—I patched together bits of clip art to create a logo that reinforces the three levels of engagement that Walt mentioned above. The logo connects mind, heart, hands, and community as best I can say it visually.

Age and health

Ben and Esther were friends of mine in their eighties when I lived in California. Going to the Gilroy Garlic Festival and stopping in town for a coffee, I saw what looked like their car, so I went up to check it out. Ben had recently left the hospital after rather serious surgery, so I didn't expect to see him out and about. Sure enough, the two were cuddled together napping on the seat like bugs in a rug.

When life gets tough, some lugs with soured mugs may be tempted to chug the jug. Alcohol is not a substitute. We need not outgrow the inner tugs for snugs and hugs. Love heals.

Parts wear out and accessories fall off. Some, like my hips, can be replaced, often with a "better than new" result, at least for the time being. But the fact of increasing mileage does not mean taking one's hands off the steering wheel and jamming the brakes. Perhaps you know someone, as indeed I did, who parked in bed for far too many of the last years of life, taking an illness or an accident, real as it may be, to define oneself as an invalid and jettison all responsibility for self-management. Drive slower. Yes, pull over when you need a nap, but keep on truckin'.

Unfinished business

Farid Elashmawi was both a colleague and friend working and writing in the field of intercultural management.[139] While his books are still read more than a decade after his untimely death, his warmth and spirit is missed. Together we shared a passion for peace in the midst of the rising animosity between the Arab world and the West. To fix and focus this passion, Farid and I struck an agreement. He would perform the hajj and I would make the pilgrimage to Santiago de Compostela. Farid completed his journey both in faith and in life, passing through both the gates of Mecca and the doors of Jannah.

Having made a good start some years ago, I am left standing at the foot of the Pyrenees, uncertain as to whether I will be able to keep on truckin' to Finisterre on foot, but convinced that by one means or another I will get there. It's on my bucket list. I owe it to Farid. I owe it to my world.

Santiago de Compostela once stood as the symbol for the Christian struggle against Islam. I and others like me want to make it a symbol of reconciliation. If we cannot eliminate the abusive sense of the words "crusade" and "jihad" we must at least bury the arms of war and allow these words to become watchwords of faith in the struggle for enlightenment and peaceful cohabitation of the planet.

 # Seven Ways to Keep on Truckin'

Now that I have reached my seventies and have supposedly gained some wisdom, I still keep looking to others for more wisdom. Many of those I've learned from are WOWs—a term I first invented to describe my wife. Rosie is a WOW—a Wiser Older Woman. I've also learned from some Wiser Older Men—and from some Wiser Younger People! Here are seven ways to keep on truckin' that I've learned from these inspiring people.

1. Keep on walking

Those wonderful figures in the R. Crumb image are definitely walking! For some years I was a runner and a backpacker. After an injury to my foot, I went back to swimming. Although I loved the relaxation, I finally accepted that I wasn't swimming fast enough to get much aerobic exercise. So I went back to my original exercise: walking.

Hills can still be a challenge to me, but as the Scottish writer Iain Banks said, "I like glen walking rather than hill walking" and here in Scotland we have as many glens as we have hills. My wife Rosie encouraged me to get serious about walking again as I prepared for yet another major operation. Walking got me fit before that operation and speeded up the recovery afterwards; walking is doing the same thing again after my most recent operation.

There are several different walks that I do right from our front door. My most frequent destination is what I call the Wallace View. As I pause to turn back home, I look many miles down the glen to the Wallace Monument, the towering memorial to William Wallace who led one of the early struggles for Scottish independence.

This walk is my thinking walk. Many times—with this book and with many previous projects—I have set off on that walk and while dodging raindrops or puddles or both, I have given my brain enough of a break that it suddenly produces the solution to a problem or the beginning of a new idea—promptly jotted down in my rain-stained wee book.

2. Keep on standing

Many years ago, someone reversed an old phrase into a powerful paradox: "Don't just do something, stand there." For decades, starting in Argentina and South Africa, groups of women have found a public place to stand together in a silent vigil. Those original groups inspired a group of women in Jerusalem (both Palestinian and Israeli) to stand as the Women in Black.

Rosie has been standing with the Women in Black in Edinburgh for more than twelve years; they stand in central Edinburgh for one hour each Saturday—in a silent vigil for peace. One of the women who inspires Rosie—and me—is Runa Mackay.[140]

Although she is now in her nineties, Runa still stands (or sometimes sits) with Women in Black. She is a very small woman who as a physician and as an activist has done very big work for the world. She went to Palestine for six months to substitute for a doctor going on leave—and she stayed thirty years. After she retired, Runa got another degree from Edinburgh and wrote a book on Palestine. And she continues to support Palestine as a key leader in Medical Aid for Palestinians.

Runa reminds me of my parents, who stood up for peace their entire lives. I remember going to a peace demonstration in the US as a young man in 1970—and meeting my parents there. Here is some of what I wrote[141] about my mother for her 80th birthday:

In the Bertolt Brecht play Mother Courage and Her Children, one of the characters says that he is angry. Mother Courage points out that it is easy to be angry. The question is: how long are you willing to stay angry? When my mother was in her twenties she was angry about the amount of money spent on war instead of peace. And she has stayed angry for sixty years.

When I was in my twenties I went downtown to a peace rally. At the train I met Mom—who was on her way to the same peace rally. In the past few years Mom and Dad have pursued their vision of world peace with visits—sometimes risky ones—to Russia, Northern Ireland, the Middle East, and Nicaragua.

Of course Mom does not look or sound angry. She does not even look courageous. She just looks like a kind white-haired lady. Which she is. But she is also a lot more than that. Her courage recalls another ancient term: witness. She would say, with Martin Luther, "Here I stand; I can do no other."

Standing for peace sometimes seems a hopeless cause. And yet, there is the starfish story. This story has emerged, through many re-tellings, from an original essay by Loren Eiseley. Here is one version:

A young man is standing on a beach looking at all the starfish left behind by the receding tide. He leans down, picks up a starfish, and throws it into the water. He moves on to the next starfish and throws it into the water too. Then an older man says to him, "But, young man, do you not realize that there are miles and miles of beach and there are starfish all along every mile? You can't possibly make a difference!" The young man picks up another starfish, throws it out into the water, and says, "I made a difference for that one."[142]

3. Keep on talking

As you have noticed by now, George and I love to tell stories. As I write this, George and I are coming to the end of six days together—just the two of us—hanging out, telling stories by the fire, and writing this book.

While we were talking over lunch just now, I realized that one of the important ways to keep on truckin' is to keep on talking and telling stories. As we become more like the people that Mark Twain described as "garrulous old men" I am less embarrassed about all the stories I have to tell. My stepdaughter Kathrine once said to me in mid-conversation, "You probably have a story about that" and then we both started laughing because I was simultaneously saying, "That reminds me of a story…"

As an old man, I can no longer walk as fast nor stand as long as I used to—but I can certainly talk just as fast and possibly talk even longer. Although not everyone is interested in the stories, I've got quite used to that; I also know that lots of other people **are** interested. And I think it is our responsibility as old guys to keep sharing our stories, to keep sharing our wisdom, to keep on talking.

My brother Giles once said that writing his newsletter was a great way to empty his brain of one idea so that there was space for another idea to emerge. That is the theme of this whole book—clearing away so that there is room for more.

The book that I wrote on influencing skills[143] has more than a hundred stories in it and this book has dozens more. So my guess is that part of being alive is noticing life around me, turning it into a story, and sharing the story with others.

4. Keep on reflecting

Talking is a way to share my thoughts and ideas with others. But I also need to reflect on my own in quiet time. Sometimes that happens in motion, while I'm out walking alone. Sometimes that happens at rest, when I'm looking out the window or sitting by the fire. And sometimes that happens while I'm writing poetry or writing in my journal.

We have already mentioned the idea of writing reflectively in a journal as you read through this book and as you move through your life. You will be less than surprised to know that I've created Seven Learnings about Journaling[144] and put those into a wee booklet on journaling. George has written a whole book on keeping a journal.

I can give you my seven learnings on journaling very quickly: *Write Now, Write Regularly, Write Irregularly, Write What I Think, Write How I Feel, Go Beyond Writing,* and *Live To Write.* You can find more details in the booklet or on my website. But the way to begin is to follow the first learning: *Write Now* and just keep on writing!

The balance of action and reflection, the balance of storytelling and journaling, the balance of walking and standing—all are part of the delicate balancing act of Trucket.

5. Keep on caring

Two years ago, I returned to the College of Wooster to work with the team of classmates planning our fiftieth reunion. My friend Lib O'Brien and I decided to visit Vi Startzman, who had been the College physician for decades. At age 98, she welcomed us graciously into her small apartment in the retirement home. She said she could only give us a few minutes because she was due at lunch soon. Then she gave us her full attention.

It was just like those few minutes of full attention that Dr. Startzman gave any of us who showed up at her doctor's office fifty years ago. I remember one time when she prescribed some medicine for the muscle spasm that was bothering me—and then provided some wisdom. She said the spasm "is a clue that will probably stay with you throughout your life; a clue that you are under stress and that you need to relax." And she was right—both about the lifetime clue and the way to resolve it!

Even after she retired as the college physician, Dr. Startzman kept working—right up to her death in her hundredth year. She set up a free clinic in Wooster, which is still flourishing, and she continued to campaign for a national health service. When we asked her what kept her so active and healthy all these years, she said *the key to living a good life is to keep on volunteering*. She inspires me as I continue volunteering my own time for the future of Wooster and for the future of Scotland.

Some years ago I began doing some training for WFP—the United Nations World Food Programme. In Thailand I met Corinne Fleischer, who was then head of the Donor Team for WFP in Asia. Corinne was intent on doing even more for WFP and she actually asked her bosses for the chance to work in Sudan. She described her job there as "feeding 3.1 million people every day" and she got me to do a few days work with her people in Darfur. That experience doubled my respect for Corinne and for the people she works with. My task was to inspire the people I worked with; their commitment to caring inspired me even more.

Now Corinne is in Rome at WFP headquarters, in charge of the entire Supply Chain for WFP. The work that she and I do with her global teams transforms individuals and inspires the whole group. Corinne keeps developing her skills as a manager and leader, she keeps inspiring her staff to make WFP's work both efficient and effective, and she keeps inspiring me to keep on caring about the people on this planet.

6. Keep on exploring

While I believe with Corinne and Runa that we need to take care of the people here on our planet, I also believe that we need to keep exploring beyond the planet so that we have a lifeboat for humanity. As a child I was inspired both by science and by science fiction to imagine going beyond this planet. As a paperboy in the 50s, I delivered my newspapers promptly every morning as soon as they arrived—except for the morning of 5 October 1957. I sat there reading all about the launch of Sputnik before I delivered the papers.

Despite my childhood dreams, I've begun to accept that I'm not likely to get anywhere near a spaceship, let alone a space station. But I have been privileged in my recent work with the European Space Agency to meet and work with two astronauts who have lived and worked on the International Space Station. Thomas Reiter and Frank De Winne are thoroughly trained, highly skilled, expert at what they do—and they are good, kind people.

Thomas and Frank are at the older end of the next generation. At the younger end of that generation is my nephew Josh, who is a Space Exploration Architect leading a team of people developing the Orion spacecraft for manned missions to the asteroids and to Mars. Josh, my friends in ESA, and thousands of other people here on Earth are making it possible for a few to begin exploring beyond. They are the kind of people I'm proud to have representing me—and the rest of humanity—as we move toward the planets and the stars. So we can all keep on exploring for generations to come.

7. Keep on keeping on

In 1972, I convinced Roy Fairfield to take me on as one of his doctoral students—even though he was already over his limit for the year. After a few weeks in his company, I just knew that he was the person who would inspire me and challenge me to learn what I wanted to learn. I don't think that either of us expected he would still be inspiring and challenging me more than 40 years later.

We first met in a month-long colloquium for doctoral students. By the end of that month of intense work and great fun, many of us felt we had been together for a year instead of a month. As Roy and I discussed this feeling, we came up with what I then decided to call the Fairfield-Hopkins Time-Stretch Phenomenon.[145] In essence, in a normal week, I might have two or three significant experiences— such as a deep conversation with a friend, an inspiring comment from a colleague, and an insightful realization during a group discussion. So that becomes my expectation of what equals a week: 3 significant experiences.

MON	TUE	WED	THU *	FRI
	*			*

But when I'm doing a workshop, or on holiday, or in some other intense and unusual experience, I might have three significant experiences in one day. I might even have three significant experiences before lunch—and three more before bedtime. And that feels like two weeks in one day!

MON	TUE	WED	THU	FRI
* * *	* * *	* * *	* * * *	* *

There is one great advantage to this phenomenon. Roy and I figure that—given the weeks and weeks of intensive workshops and other intensive experiences we have had—we have lived several hundred years already!

As George and I have noted before, time also seems to speed up as we grow older. Perhaps I could call this the Fairfield-Hopkins Time-*Shrink* Phenomenon. The best way I know to deal with the **shrinking** of time with age is to keep having those significant experiences that **stretch** time. So I continue to work, to learn, and to go on star days. "Star days" is the name that Rosie and I give to our regular days away from home when we go exploring (because we put a star on the calendar to remind us!)

Yesterday's star day included the usual amount of serendipity: a view from a thousand-year-old tower, a delicious scone with soup, and a fascinating discussion with two rangers who maintain the Fife Coastal Path on which we were walking. Three significant events— in one day.

Roy inspired me to start writing haiku, he encouraged me to teach in alternative institutions, and he challenged me to go beyond where I thought I could go. He sends out occasional Mood Pieces to keep us up to date on his doings in what he calls reFIREment—having successfully avoided retirement for decades. He often ends his messages by saying, "We keep on keeping on."

I once sent Roy a list of seven things[146] I've learned from him, but rather than give the full list here I'll point you to my website for the full message and just record the last one here:

As a HIP (Humor, Irony, Paradox) person, you balance the paradoxes of anger and calm, writing for yourself and others, working alone and in groups, exploring new possibilities and archiving old realities. You continue to be interested in what I am doing—and in what dozens of your other friends are doing. You know when to stay and when to move on. You speak of reFIREment: firing yourself up instead of tiring yourself out. But I have also learned from you that sometimes you can't wait for an organization or a system to fire you; you've got to fire yourself. And then re-fire yourself into new challenges and new possibilities.

Keep on Truckin!

A sample Trucket List

If you are wondering what your Trucket List might look like, here is
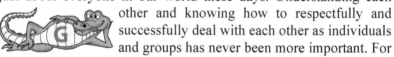
the latest version of my own Trucket List to give you an example:

Keep on writing a daily haiku
Keep on writing grooks and other poetry
Keep on writing about my Learnings
Keep on journaling
Keep on enjoying star days with Rosie

Staying LinkedIn

The cultural competence I mentioned earlier is a critical need for just about everyone in our world these days. Understanding each other and knowing how to respectfully and successfully deal with each other as individuals and groups has never been more important. For about six years now I have been the owner and manager of an online LinkedIn group for SIETAR Europa [147] discussing "Competence in Intercultural Professions." Normally this commitment costs me at least ninety minutes a day and has helped me listen to, speak to, serve, and even mentor members of the group; it is one of the most satisfying things I do.

With the learning curve and the technical challenges that social networking can pose for "digital immigrants" of my age, social networking offers those who are starting to travel less the opportunity to travel more. Some activities are more conducive to the reFIREment that Walt described earlier. My networking is one of them. Sure, there is the routine grunt work of deleting spam and the tedium of managing a database, but frequently the payoff is reconnection with old colleagues and friends.

Even more exciting is the sparkling opportunity to introduce newbies to our intercultural profession and guide them in the search for what they need to succeed. Some are fresh and fired up by studies in the field; others are looking for direction amidst career crisis or change. Most are excited by a ripe possibility for meaning and are grateful for a bit of encouragement and some tips on how to Plucket.

Collaboration for understanding each other and cohabitation of the planet and so harvesting the fruits of our diversity to meet our needs will remain critical human challenges for the foreseeable future. No one has enlightened me more in this regard than Cameroon-born Dominique Wolton, Director of the Communication Sciences Institute at the National Centre for Scientific Research in France. Wolton insists that transmitting information is not communication; rather *real communication is cohabitation*, [148] the persistent exchange and negotiation of meaning and action that allows us to live together peaceably. We've hardly started.

Whether you are an active netizen or not, this aim of cohabitation is well worth remembering and putting into practice in how you communicate with family, friends, and the rest of the world about you. Use those insights that age gives you not to be crotchety and critical, but to lend your wisdom to others, as you tend to, defend, mend, blend differences and with luck, sometimes end the pending conflicts of difference around you by what you send.

Incidentally, this same organization at its 2005 congress gave me a bit of a tucket by handing me a "lifetime achievement" award, which sits like a trophy on my desk. I was surprised, flattered—and ambivalent about how to interpret this. Was this organizational Oscar a message that said, "You've done your job, now step aside and let somebody else take over"? Or, just a friendly "Thank you."

Certainly it was the latter, but my debilitating suspicion was that it was an old guy bye-bye. That was a mental glitch that I had to deal with in order to keep on truckin' and I am happy that I did.

REFLECTION
What are the useful habits that promote your health and energize you?

What messages do you carry that debilitate rather than empower you?

How do you reframe unhelpful perceptions of old age?

How do you use yourself as an instrument and how do you keep in tune?

Which practices in this chapter appeal as possibilities for you?

What other practices do you use now or imagine using in the future?

I celebrate myself, and sing myself,
And what I assume you shall assume,
For every atom belonging to me as good belongs to you.

Walt Whitman[149]

7: The Tucket List

To tuck is to play a drum roll. A tucket is a fanfare—a trumpet blast with a roll of drums—that originated in Elizabethan drama.[150] So your Tuckets are your fanfares. Tuckets are things you are proud of, happy about, and inspired by—and things that others tell you that you have done to inspire them or make them happy.

Choosing to Tucket is choosing to toot your own horn and sound your own drum, possibly to others but mainly to yourself. It's about buoyant self-esteem, whether or not others are there to encourage you. After all, as Maxwell Maltz says, "Low self-esteem is like driving through life with your hand-brake on."[151] If that terrifying phrase, "What have I done with my life?" insinuates itself accusingly into your thinking as you age, it's time to Tucket.

Why is this important?

Marshall Rosenberg[152] suggests that the emptiness I can often feel is a result of living in a world where I am taught to define people as good guys and bad guys, where praise and blame rule, and result in

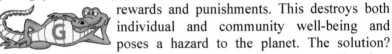 rewards and punishments. This destroys both individual and community well-being and poses a hazard to the planet. The solution?

Knowing and fulfilling my needs and yours where I can, rather than touting myself beyond credibility or accusing myself or another of falling short of standards. I feel good about myself when I remember the moments when I got my deepest needs met and helped others meet theirs. It's like a drum roll and a trumpet sounding in my heart.

Adding up our years, Walt and I have been teaching negotiation skills for well over half a century. Negotiation is a way of resolving seemingly conflicting wants by exchanging things that get each other's needs met. Two critical insights occurred to us along the way.

The first was the realization that striking a deal isn't really about offering rewards or threatening punishment to get someone to comply with what I want. We scrapped that power trip and the kind of talk that went with it. Rather, real win-win negotiation is about exchange that fills hands, minds, and hearts with satisfaction that either didn't exist before or needed to be restored. No deal is perfect, but striking a satisfying one can take us closer and invite us to create even more satisfying "arrangements" together.

A second "Aha!" in teaching negotiation and in negotiating life is that judging others, whether negatively or positively, is less than useful. Labels and judgments short-circuit the effort to identify and understand real needs—my own as well as yours—and figure out how we may fulfill them with and for each other. The key is seeing beyond my own knee-jerk inner blurting about my pleasure or pain, to what the real story line is. Like an expectant theatergoer, I come to the show with my own bottled-up normalcy. I sit clutching the program, maybe reading it or maybe jabbering with my neighbor, as I wait for the lights to dim and the curtains to open.

When the swags part, the fanfare and applause grab me from my complacent plush seat. Willy-nilly I am projected on stage. I am in the story. The players act parts of me, little or big scenes from my life. It's the fanfare, the applause, the tucket that calls me out of my somnolent self to look again at scenes from my life's drama. As my tragedy or my comedy is unmasked and played out by the cast, I am somehow made stronger and readied for what is next on the stage of life. It's called *catharsis*, emotional and spiritual cleansing. Real art, theater, cinema, the wonders of nature can all invite this.

So, Tucket is not just the rattle and the toot and the handclapping noise, but also my metaphor for the wake-up call to come to grips with my inner needs, hopes, loves, satisfactions, and desires. Tuckets in real life can be my memories, memorabilia, and memorials to how my truly human needs have been and are being met, and my determination to meet them successfully when I exit their theater for the street. They call me to gratitude, to act-knowledge-meant, to inspire me for what can be in this now and the next.

> REFLECTION
> *What do you hear from within or without that helps you feel good about yourself? What tuckets trigger your vitality and stimulate your oomph?*

Sage on the stage and Guide on the side

Before I begin sharing my seven tuckets, I want to respond to George's wonderful image of the theatre. He speaks of being pulled from the audience on to the stage. I have the same experience in the theatre—and I also have the opposite experience. I have been a performer since the age of eight, when I added a funny bit to my song recital at the Quinn School of Music—and got a laugh! I was hooked. In college I performed on stage in two Shakespeare plays and a dozen other plays. Now I perform when I demonstrate influencing skills—and tell stories—on my training courses. And I still get some laughs.

But there is a difference now. During my training courses, I don't just stand in front of people to perform. Once I've introduced the process, I kneel down beside people to coach them as they develop specific skills. As George says, I move between being a sage on the stage and a guide on the side.

When I go to the theatre, I do expect to be pulled on to the stage—and I also expect to be pulled from the stage into the audience. In my mind, I even move back and forth during the performance—

experiencing what it is like to be on the stage and what it is like to be in the audience. That's vital when I'm working with people on my courses—and vitalizing when I'm in the theatre.

One of those vitalizing moments happened in February 2003. But this story is one that really does require two background stories first. In 1964, when I was a skinny student at the College of Wooster, I played Sir Andrew Aguecheek in Shakespeare's *Twelfth Night*. My much larger friend Chuck Gabriel played Sir Andrew's partner, Sir Toby Belch.

In 2001, at our 35th college reunion, I saw Chuck approaching across the room. I hailed him: "How now, Sir Toby Belch!"

"Sweet Sir Andrew!" he replied and went right on with his speech, expecting me to know my next line. Which I did not. But we had a big hug and a great laugh. And that was that. He died a month later.

Two years later, in 2003, Rosie and I were attending a production of *Twelfth Night* by the Shakespeare's Globe Theatre. It was a very special evening because the performance was held in the Middle Temple—in the very same room where Shakespeare and his friends had presented the original production of *Twelfth Night* almost exactly 400 years earlier.

As Rosie and I took our seats, I noticed that there was an empty chair just beside us, so I said, "I wish Chuck Gabriel could be here so that Sir Toby and Sir Andrew could enjoy this together."

Rosie's response in the theatre that evening still moistens my eyes. She said: "He is here. And so are all the other Sir Tobys and Sir Andrews."

I spent that evening in the company of an enthusiastic audience enjoying great actors—and in the company of the spirits of all the other people who had ever watched the play or ever acted those parts in the previous 400 years.

My Seven Tuckets

1. Toot your own horn

Although this may go against messages from my culture and from my family upbringing, there are times when I need to blow my own trumpet and enjoy the fanfare—if not the whole fan club. I'm just chuckling to myself about this because when I was young my mother gave me the trumpet she had played as a child and it became mine. So for several years I literally did blow my own trumpet every day!

I'm a bit more modest these days, but not always. When I'm feeling good about myself, I quote Mark Twain: "I was born modest. But it wore off."[153]

Although it would be nice to think that others will always give you tuckets, my experience says that sometimes I have to do the fanfare myself. And I can toot my own horn even when no one else is around—just by writing stories like this one.

2. March to your own drum

A crucial part of the tucket is the drum as well as the trumpet. The drum roll gets attention and provides the support for the trumpet call. I see that also as the drum roll providing the context for the trumpet. And that context belongs to me. Thoreau is always worth quoting twice:

> *If a man does not keep pace with his companions, perhaps it is because he hears a different drummer. Let him step to the music which he hears, however measured or far away.*[154]

So play your own drum and live in your own way and celebrate yourself!

3. Be inspired

As my friend Dina Glouberman[155] says, "Our task here is to inspire and to be inspired." Let's start with being inspired. That provides the energy to inspire others. Each time I read what George is writing for this book, I am inspired by his stories to create inspiring stories of my own.

As I listen to the inspiring stories of WFP staff, who risk their lives to bring food to starving people, I am inspired to do what I can to support them with my skills and my donations—and to inspire others to join me in doing that.

One spring we were on our annual holiday with our grandchildren. Our second granddaughter had just turned ten and was enjoying having what she called "deep conversations" with her mother. Frances wanted to continue talking like that over dinner, so my wife asked her a good question: "Who inspires you?" Fran was walking back from the kitchen at that moment, passing behind my chair, and—as my wife told me seconds later—Fran pointed down at me. Rosie said the look of delight on Fran's face then appeared on my face. It was a magical moment that went on and on, as Fran said that her mum and her granny also inspired her.

I told that story to my friend Alan Raleigh a few weeks later and as we thought about our own answers to that question, we agreed that each of us is inspired by his wife. Both of them do magical things with people by listening to them and by asking good questions.

And just as I'm finishing this section, George walks in with the news that Pete Seeger has just died. We're both a bit choked up as we remember how many times he inspired us with his music and with his commitment. So his banjo is in the background right now as I continue to write about being inspired.

4. Inspire others

As Dina says, we are both inspired and inspiring. I think of a joyful two days at a conference that I attended last year. Among the 150 participants were a couple dozen people who had—over the past seven years—been in T Groups that I facilitated. As I walked in the door, one of those people greeted me with a grin and a big hug. Seconds later I got another grin and hug from someone else. That continued for two days: big hugs and big grins—again and again. Those people told me that they were so delighted to see me because my work with them had inspired them to do great things in their own work. They had been inspired by me to inspire others.

And the whole experience of being with those people re-inspired me for the work I was about to do. So the virtuous circle of inspiration spirals upward, carrying us all.

If you are wondering who you might inspire or how you might inspire them, you can ask yourself a very simple question: *What kind of world do you want? My* friend Jim Lord[156] has written a wonderful book with this title—and you can download it at no cost. And you can then adjust the question to other challenges. Right now I am regularly asking my college classmates: What kind of Wooster do you want? And I am also asking people in Scotland: What kind of Scotland do you want? You might ask yourself what kind of life you want, what kind of family you want, what kind of future you want. Your answers will inspire others—and you.

5. Flow with your own river
Recently, I was working for two intense days with a client from Moscow on what he wants to do with the next years of his life. We were working at my favorite venue in Scotland. Harburn House has a huge billiard table covered with boards to make a huge table. I laid out large strips of blue paper around the table and we turned that blue paper into a River of Life. On one bank we put the events of Ilya's life and on the other we put world events.

Then, using more sticky notes, Ilya filled in the four currents of the river with key moments in his Learning, Working, Playing, and Relating. And there we had it—Ilya's River of Life.

Even if you don't have a big table, you can do this on the floor—or even on a small table. Be sure to take some photos—this will be a great tucket to preserve as an emblem of all the great moments throughout your life.

6. Share past successes

When we had completed the River of Life, I asked Ilya to write a series of stories about good times in his life and together we noted the skills and values that emerged from each story.[157] We put each skill and value on a separate sticky note and covered a wall with them. Then he clustered them in groups and chose the top groups of skills.

At the end of the two days, using a template of simple questions like What and Why, he wrote out his Passionate Purpose for the next few years. And then he added some specific Serious Dreams for this year.

Although we did spend some time during the two days talking about the tough times he's had in his life, we moved beyond that to focus on success.

I still remember a stunning moment when I was first doing this kind of work in the 1970s. I was working with a young woman in her twenties who had been through lots of troubles and had worked with various other professionals before she came to me. I asked her to write her life story so that we could pull out the skills and values. Each week's story was more dismal and depressing than the previous one. She had been through tough times. One week I noticed that her new chapter had skipped a couple of years from the previous one. I was more than a bit worried by this gap and feared it might have been an even more traumatic time for her.

But I took a deep breath and decided to ask her about those missing years. "Oh, those were really good years!" When I told her that we were looking for those good times so that we could build on her past successes, she was surprised. Her response has haunted me all these years and stays with me whenever I do this work: "No one has ever wanted to know about the good years before."

7. Imagine future dreams

When you have created your own River of Life, when you have tooted your own horn and played your own drum, when you have inspired and been inspired, when you have looked at all you have done in your past successes—then you have what you need to imagine your future dreams.

This is what I call a Serious Dream.[158] That term has emerged from my favorite line: *A goal is a dream taken seriously.*

Over the years I have kept a record of some of the hundreds of Serious Dreams created by people in my workshops. Here are a few to inspire you as you develop your own Serious Dream:

Playing the piano again

> *Move in harmony toward a richer life*

> *Lead an organization to success and enjoy life*

> *To make a difference and end hunger*

> *Build a ballet school*

During the referendum campaign, I ordered a new T Shirt to wear while we had our brief Scottish summer. It plays with the word *Aye*, which we often say in Scotland when we mean Yes. We also sometimes say *Yours Aye* at the end of a message, meaning *Yours Forever*. The T Shirt says:

Aye
Have a Dream

So, yes, have a dream. And take it seriously. Forever.

A sample Tucket List

If you are wondering what your Tucket List might look like, here is the latest version of my own Tucket List to give you an example:

Celebrate the delight of my new frog avatar
Celebrate going beyond 70
Celebrate finishing this book
Celebrate our continuing campaign toward independence

My Tuckets

Gathering and hearing tuckets doesn't demand so much a special effort as a frame of mind, a kind of attention that may have to wrestle with earlier life warnings about pride and self-aggrandizement in order to take in, to feel the truly good stuff about myself that others offer me.

Being positive is essential, but takes sincerity. So don't confuse what we are saying with the current mood of compulsive positivity that declares everything "awesome," "fantastic," "outta' sight," etc. I don't buy it. Outstanding moments no longer stand out when there is no everyday foil to reflect them.

Some current research[159] even suggests that a foamy mouthful of unbridled adjectives may actually lead to depression and inferior performance. Fat flattery falls flat. The momentary pleasure of inflationary praise deflates when we sense it's only that.

Worse, the flash of such verbal bling-bling can cause us to cast a blind eye on the institutional and individual challenges and needs in and around us, and perhaps to stop the Truckin' we need to keep doing. The inflated language, the desperation to be "up" seems to have become a mandate in US English, and is globalizing. Perhaps it is symptomatic of the deep need for self-recognition and belonging going unfulfilled, hearing or giving myself or others a real Tucket when it's needed.

Culture clash

Tooting your own horn was not a praiseworthy behavior in my family. At the suspicion of self-praise, my mother would usually turn up her nose and remark aloud to no one in particular, "Something stinks around here..." My second-generation immigrant family discourse still bore the value that, "If everyone helps everyone else, everyone gets helped."

So, it was culture shock for me to enter the US mainstream as I grew up to discover that the dominant discourse was, "If everyone takes care of number one, everyone gets taken care of." To this day I am rather reticent about my accomplishments, perhaps sometimes to the detriment of effectively marketing the things that I create.

A sweet store of Tuckets

No matter, I have nonetheless a goodly "good on ya'" collection, largely from the people that I've trained, taught, mentored, or somehow assisted to realize themselves and their goals. As part of my Chucket and Shucket efforts, I have digitized the better part of my personal and family goodies collection—along with many other tangibles—making my kudos as well as my history available with a couple of taps on the face of my iPhone.

It's always there should I need a booster or want to enjoy the warm reminiscence found in a photo of collaboration or celebration. Some things, of course, submitted to being scanned, but their meaning was too intense to allow them to be discarded or even given away, at least at this point in life.

While some of my tuckets come from those letters and notes from individuals or groups that I have worked with or coached, others are simple thank-you's or details of life changes since we spent time with each other and did things together. They may be two pages long, or a few words scribbled on the back of a photo.

Re-reading them, I was aware of the warmth in my heart about needs satisfied and favors bestowed. In the words of Carter Chambers (the role played by Morgan Freeman in *The Bucket List* film), "You measure yourself by the people who measure themselves by you."[160]

Seeing myself through other eyes and creative hands

Precious in a special way are those items through which people expressed themselves in sketches, images, and paintings and then sent them to me. The walls of my apartment are covered with such creations, paintings done by friends along with memorabilia from adventures and travels, a brass plate from Sri Lanka, a war club from Fiji, carpentry tools handed on from my grandfather, an Indonesian medicine case, a mask from Haiti that brings good juju, Cathy's canvases of flowers and places, a watercolor of Granada by Mirka Molnar Lachka (one of my interns), an icon of St. George from Mount Athos, and pictures made of reindeer fur from Yakutsk, where Walt and I led a course on a boat up and down the Lena River.

Human Tuckets

For over a quarter century I have steadily had interns working in my office and most often living in my home, sometimes more than one at a time. They have come from the four corners—sixteen nations so far—and are still coming. It can be a pleasant surprise as well as a disconcerting experience to share the enthusiasm and uncover the talent of burgeoning youth.

In many cases I have been able to follow their life trajectory after leaving my little shop for their own and bigger spaces that have sometimes awed me. Tuckets: autographed copies of their books written, films produced, arts created, selfless service work, even calls to hire me!

From the outset, I learned how much learning experience an internship promises and can provide. Too often I saw places where internship meant, "Watch what we are doing, do some grunt work, and bring us coffee when we want it." The real key to satisfaction, however, lies in the mutual setting of needs into motion, which often means making them conscious and understood. When this happens both intern and mentor carry tuckets that are tickets to the future.

Some Tuckets make my nest homey

Some years ago I asked a young student of interior decorating how she would describe the style of the place I lived in. Her response: "Early ethnological museum." She was, from an outsider's professional perspective, no doubt right. But of course she could not see into the soul of the curator.

My home and my world are one, and a wee tucket sounds whenever I lift my eyes from my work and look around. My memorabilia put an upbeat spin on the meaning of "Been there, done that." Instead of signaling dismissal and boredom, for me they ring positive. They encourage me to accept a warm hug from my history and the people in it.

Also at times casting eyes on this or that little tucket reminds me to reconnect with the living as well as spirit-Skype with the dead. Both Walt and I share anecdotes about our fathers in this book—and, as we are working together, even sense their presence. I sometimes imagine the two of them as having discussions and even arguments akin to ours but with each other in some celestial café.

Enjoying your own accomplishments

When it comes to remembering my own creativity and using it as a spur to keep on truckin', I am rather lucky, as in the course of my years of work, I wrote a number of books. Not enough to fill a shelf by any means, but enough to remind me in a glance, in a tangible way, of a few of my better doings. Writing was often a collaborative effort, like writing this book with Walt.

So, the books also remind me of the people in my work and life, and recall the common pleasures of collaboration and the challenges we met together. Whatever the efforts you have engaged in, it is important not to brood over the damning question, "What do I have to show for it?" Even if your life's work was not focused on producing tangible stuff, intangibles have left their mark, memories of patient efforts to remind you of the hours and days you spent, what the energy you spent created for yourself, your family, and the rest of the world.

> REFLECTION
> *What tangible reminders do you have of the things you've accomplished thus far in your life?*
>
> *How can you shape your living space to remind yourself of what you have invested and created—even if it's not visible and tangible?*

Possession and renunciation

When it comes to staying in touch with many of our tuckets, often it seems that the material, the tangible is better. Over time, some memories fade and a certain memento may no longer be meaningful, so it may be time to chuck it, but with great care, often passing it on to a friend or relative who may have a connection with it. Making a gift of the memento in question may be a tucket for that person and also feel like a tucket to your thoughtfulness and generosity.

Should you empty your bucket ultimately by renouncing all? Becoming a sadhu or a monk is a choice that some make and, if they succeed, become in a way everyone's father or kin. Feeling the fullness in emptiness and being called *babaji* or *brother* may be the ultimate tucket.

In the end, of course, you will leave all and go lightly into that tunnel of light and ultimate enlightenment that it leads to… We don't know where, but we will all make the journey soon enough. I suspect that in some way we will take our tuckets with us to any final accounting.

How good do you feel about yourself? What makes you feel good about and right with yourself alone or as part or your family or group? Do you express that to yourself? And if so, how do you do that? Do you express that to others? And if so, how do you do that? These are all culturally delicate questions. We are aware that satisfaction in much of what we have shared above is generated by our own cultural background and experiences.

Tuckets may feel better for some of us as something we share with others as a family, group, or team. Others may want to feel that tuckets are tailored individually to celebrate their individual uniqueness. This is a cultural preference, but the important thing is the valuing of self and others that enriches our being and our being together. Bestowing credit and tuckets on others can also contribute to our sense of well being, not only to theirs.

If you come from a closely-knit culture where credit and acknowledgement belong to everybody "on the team" or from a closely-knit or very egalitarian society where standing out is immodest and brash, you will feel and express your satisfaction differently. Some of us are brought up to believe that it is the "squeaky wheel that gets the grease," while others of us are cautioned that "it is the duck that quacks first that gets shot," or, "tall poppies will be cut down to size."

In a world where globalization is a phenomenon to be reckoned with, we see the extremes of competition, jingoism, personal branding, and marketing madness. We can only encourage you to enjoy the pleasure of being with yourself and others as best suits your environment and your spirit. Your tuckets may suggest that you have you something to market, but that is another business.

> *REFLECTION*
> *What are the appropriate and acceptable ways—given the culture of your family, time, and place—to relish your own tuckets and offer tuckets to others?*

We suspect that if you have been both reading and reflecting, as well as making notes for yourself, letting the suggestions in this book play out for you and meet your needs, you deserve a tucket not just from us but from yourself. We suspect that you may have or soon will have experienced some of the same enrichment of life in doing these exercises as we did in doing them as we were writing about them. Life got better for us as well as for those around us. Congratulations! Keep dipping into your bucket for the goodies that you find there.

Tucket as an antidepressant?

Down in the blues? It may seem bizarre, but it seems that depression is on the rise, particularly among younger people in developing countries that are enjoying an economic boom time. China, in particular, is experiencing an epidemic right now—it is also a boom time for shrinks and pharmaceuticals.

For younger folks it seems to be a paralysis that sets in when they compare themselves negatively with others who've been more successful than they have been. Worse, perhaps than the depression itself, is the antidote of Schadenfreude, taking delight in the misfortunes of others, with its miserable side effects. That can occur at any age, but it is more prone to happen when we are feeling low about ourselves, alone and helpless.

Tucket is my way of encouraging myself to affirm and give credit as best fits my sense and your scene, to be accepting and grateful for what has been, before I rush to what is next, or worse, settle into the gloom that there is nothing next. Old age is neither valued nor of interest to many around us. So, appreciating where I have been and what I have done can help me avoid or even pitch the pills.

The poet Yevgeny Yevtushenko asserted that character begins to build at the first twinge of dissatisfaction with ourselves, and further that, "Only when the sense of the pain of others begins does man begin."[161] Both true, *and* I'm in better shape to ask "what's next" fortified by my tuckets. It is nice to know that somebody "up there"

or "out there" loves me, but even more encouraging to realize from time to time who it is, and how and why.

Prompts
We are all on stage in the theatre of life, so here are some prompts, leading lines for giving tuckets to yourself and others:

- *"I remember when I/you/we..."*
- *"Sure, I/you/we can..."*
- *"It/you really made a difference when..."*
- *"It was a gift to me/us, when you..."*
- *"What a brave/generous/etc., step..."*
- *"Here's what I/you/we learned when..."*

> REFLECTION
> *Imagine your life as a river, flowing down from ancestral mountains, sometimes smoothly, sometimes turbulent with cataracts and falls, swelled by the rains of experience, enriched by the tributaries of others' lives flowing into yours, a river that buoys up and carries the ships and skiffs of everyday activities and that irrigates the lands along its course to the embracing and eternal sea. Imagine. Enjoy. Capture. Share.*

A goal is a dream taken seriously.

Walt Hopkins[162]

Beyond the ...ucket Lists

Farewell

George and I began this project in the spring of 2013 when work was at a standstill for me. Perhaps that's why I was thinking of just saying *Fucket* to my work. Then, like the proverbial London bus that never shows until three come along at once, three of my clients sprang into action—simultaneously. I went into *Plucket* mode and grabbed at all three opportunities.

In July I sent a *Tucket* message to my friends to share my delight with all three clients and to describe the series of amazing workshops that I'd done with wonderful people.

In August I had to send another kind of message; I had just been diagnosed with prostate cancer. I was determined to keep on truckin' but the *Trucket* approach required a lot more effort than usual. And it took me some time to accept that the *Ducket* approach was not going to make the cancer go away.

When my mind was unable to focus on anything else I went into *Chucket* mode. I went out to the garage and opened one of the dozen file drawers that I'd been meaning to clear—someday. In a single day, I cleared almost an entire drawer of receipts, invoices, and bank statements going back to the 1970s. I continued chucking stuff both before and after the surgery. I've now cleared more than five file drawers and the process continues.

When I've cleared that stuff, then I'll start working on other projects—like the updated Castle poster—so that I can chuck all the files in those file drawers. That way George can relax a bit too. As we are literary executors for each other, one of us is going to be stuck with a lot of work unless we both keep on with the *Chucket*!

The cancer diagnosis, the surgery, and now the recovery have all provided plenty of opportunity for the *Shucket* approach—the important things become more important and the rest gets shucked away.

So, for the past two years, I have been living what George and I have been writing about—learning more about all seven ...ucket ways by using each ...ucket way in my own life.

I have kept the *Tucket* way going in the past few months—for others as well as myself—by signing more than sixty Dream Cheques to encourage others in their Serious Dreams. A Dream Cheque is a gift of ten pounds to encourage you to take your dream seriously. I started working with people on their Serious Dreams more than 35 years ago and since 1982 I have written more than 600 Dream Cheques.

If a Serious Dream sounds just a wee bit like a Bucket List, I suppose you could call it a single-item version. One of my Serious Dreams is: *encouraging people to change their world and change their lives—one serious dream at a time.*

So, now that you have read about, written about, and talked about the seven ways of clearing and filling your life with the ...ucket Lists, you might even want to create a Bucket List—or a Serious Dream.

If you do create a Serious Dream, I'd be happy to hear what it is. In order to maintain my own commitments—I *am* learning to Ducket sometimes—I won't promise to respond to each of you. But I do promise to send a Dream Cheque to at least one person each month—and you might be the one. Write your Serious Dream in a maximum of ten words and include the name you use when you deposit a cheque in the bank. Dream seriously!

Adieu

Apparently it was a golfer who first said, "the harder I practice, the luckier I get." Luck is perhaps too rarely associated with old age going forward. It is easy to use luck as an excuse rather than as a plaudit. We sometimes hesitate to give ourselves tuckets for the high moments in our past with words such as, "Well, I was really lucky that..." Or, "I sure lucked out when..." Modesty, of course, perhaps not to impose on others. But, I can say, "How very lucky I have been."

Perhaps this is so because I was "lucky" enough to have inherited and watered certain seeds planted in me via childhood religious instruction, belief that was modeled by parents and family. "Do everything with thanksgiving," [163] was a consistent theme, a shortened mandate of a biblical exhortation. Thankfulness reduces anxiety and promotes happiness, not just self-satisfaction, but outpouring.

> *Give, and it will be given to you. A good measure, pressed down, shaken together and running over, will be poured into your lap. For with the measure you use, it will be measured to you.*[164]

It's my hope that what we have shared here will lead you to thankfulness about what has been and what is to come. It is, as Brother David, whom I spoke of earlier, has argued, the key to happiness.

Grieving is a kind of thanksgiving

It would seem then that the advice to *chuck out something* would come as second nature to us men, practiced as we are in abandoning the here and now for some future bigger win or gain, whose luster is quickly tarnished as we are urged to leave it behind and move on. It's always a new season. Laurels fade and are to be forgotten, not rested upon.

However, what we're talking about here and now is not the culturally coerced set of male sacrifices that are taken for granted, rarely examined, and simply expected of us. Nor are we talking about the reluctant sacrifices we make and take as normal. Rather, as we home in on the purpose of our lives, a process abetted by ageing, we are encouraged to take a second look at what we have sacrificed for, what we have given away in order to have what we have.

Chucket, our starting point, and the subsequent chapters—Shucket, Ducket and Fucket—were in fact important paradoxical ways of shedding the irrelevant and regaining ourselves, taking back losses that we have been consciously or unconsciously grieving over for much of our lives. Grief is not automatic. It is something we need to allow ourselves to have or it too will be taken away from us. Grief leads to the joy of possessing ourselves and embracing each other, no matter what we lament as having been despoiled of.

This book has been about managing loss and gain, so that we can be "Surprised by Joy—impatient as the wind."[165] The poet Robert Bly insists that the principal male emotion is grief. The man, to be a man, at least culturally if not biologically, must, whether he likes it or not, let go of things. He is told to stop playing and go to work. He is inducted into the military, or spends years making choices that allow him to avoid this fate.

He works to support a family, which in many cases he has little or no time to enjoy. He lets go of the woman who accuses him of neglect. If he belongs to a rejected minority for his color, ethnicity, or lifestyle orientation, his losses may seem doubled. His pleasures and orgasms are brief and fleeting.

Yes, we men are brought up to drop our load and run onto the next thing. To not notice the plundering of spirit and life, we are encouraged to think of ourselves as heroic, winners, for playing the game rightly. Even the prizes are often disappointing.

The emotion that accompanies and follows giving away and losing his life is one of grief and a man must learn to grieve to find his joy. In my years of doing workshops for men, I became aware that tears for many men, rare as they are, are even more rarely tears of joy. Such men create camaraderie to face the enemy in real life and its simulation in sport and its dreadful execution in war. They cry for fallen buddies, not for themselves.

Aeneas in exile—as so many men feel themselves to be—remembering his comrades exclaims, *"Sunt lacrimae rerum et mentem mortalia tangent."* "The world is a world of tears, and the burdens of mortality touch the heart."[166] When they succeed in the battle for great success, power, and wealth it may seem more like running away from death than toward life—many of us keep on running until our legs buckle under us. We are taught "not to cry over spilt milk" and that sportsmanship is about accepting a loss and coming back to fight again.

Grieving is waking up to the loss and accepting it. It is not a time for blaming ourselves. Rather it is the emotion that connects us to our needs and allows us to let go of moments in which we experienced them without fulfillment. Gordon Clay, whom we mentioned earlier, brought men together in a process he called "Healing the Father Wound." He helped men to come to grips with what so many in our generation experienced, the absence of our fathers and our alienation from them.

Accepting father and their father's often unrequited love allows men to remove themselves from the mortal competition that they frequently wage with each other. It makes close male friendship and sharing possible and desirable. In our pain many of us were brought up to see father as the problem and to "run to mother," find a woman to listen, often endangering the relationship with the woman we are committed to. In our men's work we embrace the motto, "Tell it to a man!" That is what we have been doing in these pages and what we urge you to do as well.

Women sometimes wonder why some men, for all their bravado are attached to what seems to be little, insignificant, or faulty: the holiness of a tattered shirt, reverence for a dirty, scuffed pair of sneakers, the halo surrounding our small box of tools. And so, sacred or profane, out of love or out of fear, we accumulate what others want and recognize as important, at the same time that we attribute meaning to what looks meaningless to them. Things that provide familiarity and companionship when companions don't.

We learn early on that there are trade-offs to be made in order to find, gain, or keep what little we really want. In the struggle to have enough resources to become free, too often things we own wind up owning us.

Men are allowed to go hunting and fishing because the world sees it as a productive behavior, leisure-time work with a payoff, the catch. Night fishing is "moonlighting." Marie Curie, observed that, "Humanity certainly needs practical men, who get the most out of their work, and, without forgetting the general good, safeguard their own interests. But humanity also needs dreamers, for whom the disinterested development of an enterprise is so captivating that it becomes impossible for them to devote their care to their own material profit." Fishing is a time for dreams.

We could not grieve, if we had not experienced the richness of that for which we grieve, so in a sense, grieving is at the root of our thankfulness for what has been and the starting point for serious dreams. Gordon Livingstone reminds us that the concept of "closure" is junk psychiatry. Even when our grieving is done, the love of one lost still lives in memory and devotion to that person and their meaning for our life and our world.

The joy of cut & paste:
Baring's daring tearing, pairing, sharing, and caring
Not all thanksgiving is grieving. A lot of it comes of giving, generosity, the delight of transferring or sharing our claim on something we love to someone we love. Dare to share what you

bear, your daily fare—it's the way you care and it makes your lair lighter and paradoxically someone else's as well. A book that I have kept at arm's reach throughout my life was born of a habit of sharing.

An English man of letters, Maurice Baring had the habit of tearing up his books, pairing related snippets to each other, and pasting them into what we used to call scrapbooks to share with friends the delicious things he stumbled upon.

Cut-and-paste was not virtual in the 1930's. It was scissors, paper, gluepot, and post. Perhaps it felt more meaningful then, as it cost more effort to search and tear out the good stuff and ready it to go. It made the literary detective more reflective and selective than click and tweet does today.

The book in my hand, one of Baring's "scrapbooks", was a published version of his bounty. Baring imagines himself at death, crossing the river Styx when Charon the boatman, acting as the customs officer of Hades, asks the question that became the title of the book, *Have You Anything to Declare?*[167]

Baring's response is the ensuing collection of the poems and prose patches that he has treasured in life. At the start of this book, we mentioned, "you can't take it with you." But, in a sense, you can. Like the recipes in my mother's cut-and-paste cookbook, treasures of the spirit do not suffer financial crises. Their value grows each time they are served up and graciously shared with others.

Like Baring, Walt and I have tried to share, often in the inspiring words of others, the ideas and feelings we have found precious and which lent meaning to the bent of our lives. Both of us come from a very litigious society where "possession is nine points of the law" and writers are terrorized into compulsive footnoting and permission seeking. It is difficult to be creative and generous when the ogre of copyright anxiety is peeking over one's shoulder.

We have tried to write this book with a different frame of mind. Yes, we have added notes at the end of the book with further information and with our sources, but we choose to see these as Tuckets of gratitude, thanksgiving, and recognition for the generous fellow travelers who helped us shuck banality and penetrate the essence of living. We gift them to you in the hope that you will both savor them and pass the plate on to others.

In France, people used to bid each other farewell with the word, *adieu*. Perhaps commending the other person to God's care was a better fit in more unsure or perilous or religious times. Today our goodbyes (a run-together form of a similar wish: "God be with ye") are much more the equivalents of "Until later…" or "See you soon." In any case, we wish you well as you go forward and hope that perhaps we will see you for real or at least online.

Our do-it duet finale
We have shared our own stories about what we have chucked or shucked or whatever. Our stories are examples, not expectations. It's not what *we* have chucked that is important; it is what *you* are going to chuck.

We look forward to seeing you online,[168] where we will go *beyond the …ucket lists* to look at the ways we've left out here, such as Lucket, Mucket, Pucket, Qucket, Sucket, Snucket, Stucket, and Yucket. We hope that you will Lucket evermore in the days to come as you use the ideas in this book in the ways that best suit your life and how you want to Trucket.

Or, if this book doesn't work for you, well, Fucket. Take the book and Chucket.

There will of course be down moments when the bucket already feels empty, as rapper A$AP Rocky1 sings:

I wonder if they miss me, as long as I make history.
Now my soul is feeling empty tell the reaper come and get me.[169]

In those moments you might get discouraged, momentarily depressed or pity yourself—but turning to these ...ucket ways will help you look carefully for what is still in the bucket.

This book is about living fully while also emptying the bucket completely before you kick it. Nikos Kazantzakis, in his stunning sequel to Homer's *Odyssey*, describes the death of Odysseus.[170] Kazantzakis imagines the moment of death as the space between the wick and the flame—the emptiness that remains after living a full life:

> *As a low lantern's flame flicks in its final blaze*
> *then leaps above its shriveled wick and mounts aloft*
> *brimming with light, and soars toward Death with dazzling joy,*
> *so did his fierce soul leap before it vanished in air.*

Notes
Sources, Attributions, and further Contributions

We have grouped these Notes by chapter so that you can find them more easily. You can track them by using the numbers or you can look below for the word, the phrase, or the name that you want more information on. This word, phrase, or name will be in **boldface.**

When one of us owns the actual book that is the source of a quotation, we give you the details of the book itself; otherwise we give you the source where we found the quotation.

If you are not interested in these Notes, just skip them. We like to give credit to others both for their ideas and for their well-written expression of ideas. One of our friends thought we might be name-dropping—but we prefer to think of it as *name-raising*. We are raising the names of people who have helped us learn. That's why you find so many people listed here and in the acknowledgements: we have learned a lot from a lot of people!

Introduction

[1] **How old would you be if you didn't know how old you are?**
Satchel Paige is probably the greatest baseball pitcher of all time. Because he was black, his entry into the Major Leagues was delayed until he was in his forties, when he joined the Cleveland Indians in 1948 and helped them win the pennant. George and Walt both grew up as fans of the Cleveland Indians. George could give you the 1948 lineup and Walt could give you the 1954 lineup. Another of Satchel Paige's great lines was this one: "Don't look back. Something might be gaining on you." For more about this amazing man, see the official website at
http://www.satchelpaige.com/quote2.html

[2] **A man needs a little madness**
Nikos Kazantzakis (1883-1957) wrote philosophy, novels, and poetry—
including a stunning sequel to Homer's *Odyssey*. He is best known for
Zorba the Greek, translated by Carl Wildman, Faber & Faber, 1961.

Our opening quotation is from the film of *Zorba the Greek*, directed by
Michael Cacoyannis and starring Anthony Quinn as Zorba. Michael
Cacoyannis wrote the screenplay, so this line is his conflation of several
lines on pages 303-304 of the novel. Zorba seems larger than life, but he
is based on Nikos Kazantzakis's friend Giorgis Zorbas.

Walt's note: In 1964, the year that the film of *Zorba the Greek* appeared,
I was visiting the home of Andrew Freris, who had been my Greek
exchange student brother during our senior year of high school two years
earlier. One evening we began discussing Zorba, and I was stunned
when Velisarios Freris, Andrew's father, calmly commented that he had
met Zorba. I love it that the original Zorba's name was George, because
George and I have been living that film for nearly forty years!

[3] **Kick the bucket**
No one knows where the phrase *Kick the Bucket* started, but it has been
used in English since the 16th century as a slang euphemism for dying.

[4] **A bucket list**
The term *Bucket List* was created by screenwriter Justin Zackham for the
2007 film *The Bucket List* that then popularized the term. The film stars
Morgan Freeman as Carter and Jack Nicholson as Edward, with
direction by Rob Reiner. Here is the line as it appears in the film:

EDWARD
It was on the floor. I didn't know it was a State secret.

CARTER (sighs)
*My freshman philosophy professor assigned this exercise in forward
thinking. We had to make a list of all the things we dreamed of doing
with our lives before we...*

EDWARD
... before you "kick the bucket." Cutesy.

And here is an excerpt from an interview with Justin Zackham:

Oh, absolutely. The thing I want to say also about the movie is that it ultimately is not about the list. The one thing that those two guys don't have on the list, which is the one thing they really get, is a best friend. They don't put it down, but yet at the end they've got someone who loves them, who they've been through this experience with. They've taught each other. They've grown from it. And the thing for me is the line that really started the script for me. Morgan says in the opening voiceover that you measure yourself by the people who measure themselves by you. I wrote that about my group of friends. And sort of just like Rob said, are you doing the best with the people who love you and who you love in the world. Everything else on the list, that's driving yourself, but to me that's what the movie's about. We talked about that over and over and that's really what the spirit of it is.

You can find the complete interview at:
http://cinema.com/articles/5504/bucket-list-the-rob-reiner-and-justin-zackham-q-and.phtml

[5] Yoda
This statue of Yoda, the familiar character of *Star Wars* film fame, was welded together from carefully collected bits of metal as sustainable art by the artist Didier Charpy, who is George's neighbor.

[6] Before the bucket you kick
This grook (a form of poetry developed by Piet Hein) is by Walt.

[7] Keep on Truckin'
Keep on Truckin' (as in "keep on moving") is a phrase that became famous from a cartoon drawn by Robert Crumb, first published in *Zap Comix* in 1968. The phrase apparently originated in a blues song sung by Blind Boy Fuller in the 1930s.
http://en.wikipedia.org/wiki/Blind_Boy_Fuller

[8] Basho, the Japanese master of haiku
Matsuo Basho was a Japanese poet of the seventeenth century Edo Period who became a master of the Japanese verse form called the haiku and worked with other men on collaborative poems. We both write haiku

and we share them with each other. We use the 5-7-5 format adapted
from the Japanese into English—as Walt explains in a haiku:

Five sounds on first line
Seven sounds on second line
Five sounds on third line

The 5-7-5 format equates Japanese sounds with English syllables, so you
just count the syllables. You might also want to hint at the season, move
from the microcosmic to the macrocosmic, pivot at the end of the second
line into a different meaning—or just ignore all those hints and write
haiku your own way.

As George says:

Birds leave tracks in sand.
We send each other pixels.
Life is short! Share joys!

Whether you write to others or treasure the words for yourself, whatever
you want to focus on, in you or around you, you can see it more clearly
and relish it by engaging in what "real men" in the past called, "the
manly love of poetry."

Exchanging haiku has become a popular activity for many people. Some
have been inspired by Denis Thériault's magical novel, recommended to
Walt almost simultaneously by two German-speaking Italian friends,
Ursula and Ruth.

Thériault's original title is *Le Facteur Émotif*, the English title is *The
Postman's Round,* and Ursula tells us that the title in German means "17
syllables of eternity."

For more on Matsuo Basho, see
http://en.wikipedia.org/wiki/Matsuo_Bash%C5%8D

You can read some of Basho's haiku in *Basho: Haiku*, translated by
Lucien Stryk, Penguin 60s Classics, 1995.

[9] **Arithmodigmaphilia (a love of number patterns)**
If you would like to read any of the Arithmodigmaphilia messages that Walt created (beginning on the first day of 2001 on 01-01-01) you can find them at
http://www.walthopkins.com/en/writings/arithmodigmaphilia/

[10] **Justin Zackham's great script**
See the note for page 1 on **a bucket list**

[11] **Echoing the Stoic philosopher Seneca**
Dale Dauten quotes Seneca and then comments on the quote: "*It is not the man who has too little who is poor, but the one who hankers after more.* It was the *hankering* that offended Seneca. He understood a concept almost lost to us: *enough.*" See:
http://www.dauten.com/stoic.html

[12] **National Men's Resource Center**
The National Men's Resource Center's website has been a treasure trove of information, insights, and services for men of all ages:
http://www.menstuff.org/frameindex.html

[13] **Procul Harum**
Just in case your memories of the 1967 Summer of Love have grown a bit faint (or never existed) you can read more about Procul Harum at
http://en.wikipedia.org/wiki/A_Whiter_Shade_of_Pale and in any case, you might want to listen again to "A Whiter Shade of Pale" by downloading it.

[14] **Serendipity**
Horace Walpole, an 18th century English author and historian, coined the word "serendipity" from the setting of a Persian fairy tale *The Three Princes of Serendib*. The island of Serendib is today's Sri Lanka.

The original story of the three princes (which is probably more than a thousand years old) includes a wonderful sequence in which they deduce a detailed description of a camel they have never seen. Voltaire's version of the story in his novel *Zadig* inspired Edgar Allan Poe to invent a deducing detective—leading to Arthur Conan Doyle's invention and others.

Walpole wrote that the three princes were "always making discoveries, by accidents and sagacity, of things which they were not in quest of." The word serendipity is often used only to refer to discovery by accident. But Walpole also included sagacity. So serendipity examples such as the discovery of penicillin or the creation of the sticky note require both chance and wisdom to notice the significance of the chance.

This book emerged from the chance of Walt playfully rhyming Bucket List with Fucket List—and the sagacity of George recognizing the potential for a book. We hope you will find serendipity here as you accidentally discover ideas that you can wisely choose to use in your own life.

[15] When you come to a fork in the road
Lawrence "Yogi" Berra was the long-time catcher and then manager of the New York Yankees baseball team. He is famous for his bewildering aphorisms. He said this one while giving teammate Joe Garagiola directions to his house. Yogi Berra, *The Yogi Book*, Workman Publishing, 1998, page 48.

[16] Echoing Siggy Freud
The father of psychotherapy, Sigmund Schlomo Freud insisted that repressed memories caused hysteria—by implication female! As men entering our penility, it is important to acknowledge what may be repressed for us and turn it into what we need to erect now.

[17] We have created an online site
Our online site will include a blog in which we continue to muse on the …ucket lists and their implications for lightening and enlightening our lives before we kick the bucket. We welcome your comments on the blog—and on this book. Clog our blog at
https://www.facebook.com/bucketbookviews

[18] Rumi
The 13th century poet Jalaluddin Rumi has reappeared in our times, translated by several people, including the contemporary poet, Robert Bly, activist leader of the mythopoetic men's movement, best known for his book, *Iron John: A Book about Men*. Rumi was reputed to create and speak poems as he danced.

The specific poem we are referring to begins this way:

Out beyond ideas of wrongdoing and rightdoing,
there is a field. I'll meet you there.

This is on page 36 of *The Essential Rumi*, translated by Coleman Barks with John Moyne, Penguin, 1995. To hear Coleman Barks reading the poem, go to http://www.poetshouse.org/watch-listen-and-discuss/listen/coleman-barks-rumi-wrongdoing-rightdoing

[19] **Kermit (Jim Henson's Muppet creation of Sesame Street fame)**
Walt's note: My niece Amanda gave me my first Kermit puppet for Christmas in 1981 when we were both much younger. That one is almost worn out, but friends later gave me two more. So one always travels with me while the others stay in my study. In gratitude for all the joy that Kermit has given me over the years, I have contributed to the wonderful work of Sesame Workshop. Here is what they do:

Sesame Workshop, the nonprofit organization behind Sesame Street, has been making a difference in children's lives for over 44 years. We use media as a tool to help children around the world reach their highest potential. When you contribute to Sesame Workshop, you are helping to spread laughter and learning to children everywhere.
http://www.sesameworkshop.org/partners/donate-2/

[20] **Showing people how to use a personal journal**
George's book on journaling is *Keeping Your Personal Journal*, Ballantine Books, 1978. Walt's booklet on journaling is *Journaling in Small Groups*, NTL Institute, 2006. We aim to have both of them available online soon—so contact us via https://www.facebook.com/bucketbookviews and we will get the links to you.

[21] **The Western Reserve**
The lands of the Connecticut Western Reserve—in what is now the Midwest of the US—were distributed to Revolutionary War veterans and to Connecticut settlers who had lost their homes during the war.

²² **Pain is inevitable. Suffering is optional.**
Haruki Murakami, *What I Talk About When I Talk About Running*,
Doubleday, 2007. See http://www.goodreads.com/work/quotes/2475030

²³ **The practical matter of winding up your affairs**
In early drafts of this book, we pointed you to an appendix on the
practical aspects of preparing for death. Rather like Walt's appendix
(which swelled, burst, and has now been chucked) the appendix on
preparing for death got too big for this book. So here we offer you one
example and one book.

The New Natural Death Handbook, edited by Nicholas Albery and
Stephanie Wienrich of the Natural Death Centre. Walt has the third
edition, published in 2000, with twenty pages of resources such as books
and videos. The book is now in its fifth edition, so you may want to go
to the website for the latest information: http://www.naturaldeath.org.uk

Walt's example: *I'm sitting at my desk, typing this note. Under my desk
is a file cabinet. The top drawer has a label that used to read: IF I DIE.
About twenty years ago I changed that label to read: WHEN I DIE.*

*The file drawer has all sorts of information that will be useful to my
family and to my legal executors—ranging from a copy of my will to
clues about my online passwords.*

*The first hanging file contains the following folders: Organ Donation:
Yes; Last Will; Living Will; Possibilities to Inherit; Memorial Service;
and Funeral Plans (which includes information on my prepaid funeral
plan and my purchased woodland burial site). The very first folder is
called READ THIS NOW and contains what in Scotland is called
Informal Writings.*

*This is a detailed memo that I first wrote in December 1981 and that I
have been revising regularly ever since. The fourteen pages give details
on Organ Donation, Will, Living Will, Power of Attorney, Life
Assurance, Where Things Are, Where Things Go, and Thoughts for a
Memorial Service. So that's what I've done to prepare the way. It's
never enough, but each bit of preparation will make things easier for
those who clean up after we're gone.*

[24] **Your old men shall dream dreams**
Joel 2:28, *The Holy Bible*, Revised Standard Version, Thomas Nelson & Sons, 1953.

[25] **A goal is a dream taken seriously**
A Goal Is A Dream Taken Seriously: The Castle Approach to Career and Life Design by Walt Hopkins, Organization Design and Development, 1986. The image of the castle and the words *A Goal Is A Dream Taken Seriously* are both © 1986, 2005 by Walter Painter Hopkins.

[26] **John Crystal and Dick Bolles**
Where Do I Go From Here With My Life? by John C. Crystal and Richard N. Bolles, Ten Speed Press, 1974, and *What Color Is Your Parachute? A Practical Manual for Job-Hunters and Career-Changers* (2013 Edition: Revised and Updated Annually) by Richard N. Bolles, Ten Speed Press, 2012.

Back in the mid-70s, Walt spent a fascinating evening with John Crystal and did the first of three two-week workshops with Dick Bolles. Walt's own work in life and career designing—see the note above—builds on what he learned from Dick and from John.

[27] **If you don't think men can bitch**
Walt first wrote about bitching by men in his article on *Househusbandry* published in *The Humanist*, May-June 1973 issue. Although bitch is unkind and inappropriate when used as a noun about one gender, it is quite accurate when used as a verb to describe how both genders can complain.

[28] **In the short run we are still alive**
John Maynard Keynes was probably the most influential economist of the 20th century—and he came back into fashion in the 2008 crash. His point about the short run and the long run is in an article that he wrote for the *New Statesman* of 10 July 1937. The article is reprinted in the centenary issue of the *New Statesman*, 12-25 April 2013, page 45.

²⁹ **Roots and Wings**
A well-known combination of these two words goes this way: "We give our children just two things—one is roots and the other is wings." We are still tracing the original source, which may be Henry Ward Beecher. If you have a definite source, we would appreciate hearing from you!

Walt's note: My sisters like the image of Roots and Wings so much that they have used it as the title of their new book, which tells the story of our parents growing up, falling in love, beginning a lifelong commitment to peacemaking, and raising the five of us children to honour our roots and spread our wings. You can find their book online in paperback or digital version as **Roots and Wings in the 20th Century: A Partnership of Family, Speaking, Writing, and Peace** by Frances Hopkins Irwin and Angene Hopkins Wilson.
http://www.amazon.co.uk/Roots-Wings-20th-Century-Partnership/dp/150555635X/ref=sr_1_6_twi_2_pap?s=books&ie=UTF8&qid=1436026947&sr=1-6&keywords=roots+and+wings

³⁰ **Notre Dame**
Though Notre Dame is known from its football squad as "The Fighting Irish" it was actually born when determined French Missionaries fought the cold and emptiness of the Midwest plains to create a school in the wilderness in the 1840's. The Notre Dame student body became largely populated by the children of the two million Catholic immigrants driven from Ireland by the potato famine in that same decade.

³¹ **Deauville**
Deauville figured prominently in *A Man and a Woman*, a 1966 French film written and directed by Claude Lelouch. And creating this footnote led us to discover that we both love this film!

³² **La Napoule**
Apparently the Greek sailors of classical times ran short of imaginative names for the colonies they settled. La Napoule, like Naples in Italy was simply called "New Town" (ΝΕΑΠΟΛΙΣ = Neapolis).

³³ **A man's a man for a' that**
A Man's A Man for A' That is the title of a poem by Robert Burns, originally published in 1786 in the collection *Poems, Chiefly in the*

Scottish Dialect, now known as the Kilmarnock Edition. Our source is *The Penguin Book of Scottish Verse* edited by Tom Scott, Penguin, 1970. To hear the most remarkable rendition of this song, follow this link to hear Sheena Wellington singing it on the day when the Scottish Parliament was reconvened in 1999—after a recess of 292 years: https://www.youtube.com/watch?v=hudNoXsUj0o

[34] **We shall not cease from exploration**
Little Gidding, from *Four Quartets* by T. S. Eliot, in *The Complete Poems and Plays 1909-1950* by T. S. Eliot, Harcourt, Brace, & World, 1952.

[35] **Campaigning for an independent Scotland**
You may be wondering why this statement is in the present tense. When we started the Yes campaign in 2012, we had roughly 30% of the vote. On 18 September 2014, we got 45% of the vote. In the continuing Yes Campaign, we think of that additional 15% as having got us to base camp. The summit is now in view and next time we will reach it!

[36] **Heard messages from our culture**
George and his colleague Eun Kim have teamed up to identify the core US values as part of the intercultural learning tools set, *The Cultural Detective®*. See http://www.culturaldetective.com/package.shtml#USA

[37] **Time you enjoy wasting**
A line by British novelist Marthe Troly-Curtin from her novel *Phrynette Married*, Macmillan, 1912.
http://www.goodreads.com/author/show/5784244.Marthe_Troly_Curtin

Chapter 1: The Chucket List

[38] **Small Boy**
Norman MacCaig, *The Poems of Norman MacCaig*, edited by Ewen McCaig, Polygon, 2005. This poem is on page 454.

³⁹ **The Complete Walker**
For those of you who love walking as much as we do, hang on to the original 1968 edition, or get the latest edition: *The Complete Walker IV* by Colin Fletcher and Chip Rawlins, Knopf, 2002.

⁴⁰ **If you wish to travel far and fast**
This quotation is attributed to Cesare Pavese, who was an anti-fascist Italian poet, novelist, literary critic, and translator.

⁴¹ **Something to eat and knitting needles**
Urszula Muskus, *The Long Bridge: Out of the Gulags*, Introduced by Peter Muskus, Sandstone Press, 2010.

⁴² **Letting go and holding on**
This quotation is attributed to Henry Havelock Ellis (1859-1939). He was a British physician, writer, and social reformer who studied human sexuality. http://en.wikipedia.org/wiki/Havelock_Ellis

⁴³ **One of my men's workshop participants**
For a number of years in the 1970's George teamed up with Phil McCrillis at the Hidden Valley Center for Men to deliver workshops for men under the title of *"How to Love an Angry Woman,"* (*"Wie liebt Mann eine Wütende Frau"* in Germany) assisting guys to deal with the feminist burst of that period. Their methodology was reflected in the book *Men and Women, Partners at Work*.
http://www.amazon.com/Men-Women-Partners-Work-Fifty-Minute/dp/1560520094

⁴⁴ **Of the making of books, there is no end**
This is the *Bible in Basic English* translation of Ecclesiastes 12:12
We will use various translations of the *Bible* for our references.

⁴⁵ **As we age and sage...everyday monks and mystics**
This line reflects two approaches to grace-full living: Marsha Sinetar's *Ordinary People as Monks and Mystics: Lifestyles for Spiritual Wholeness*, Paulist Press, 1986, and Zalman Schachter-Shalomi, *From Age-ing to Sage-ing: A Profound New Vision of Growing Older*, Grand Central, 1995.

[46] Pareto would have been happy
Vilfredo Pareto was an early 20th century Italian economist and philosopher who observed that approximately 80% of effects or results come from 20% of the causes.
http://en.wikipedia.org/wiki/Vilfredo_Pareto

[47] Zeno's paradox
Zeno's paradoxes are a set of philosophical problems devised by the Greek philosopher Zeno of Elea (ca. 490-430 BC).
http://en.wikipedia.org/wiki/Zeno's_paradoxes

[48] Simplify, simplify
Henry David Thoreau, *Walden*, first published in 1854. This line comes in Chapter 2. An annotated version online is the source we can now recommend: http://thoreau.eserver.org/walden02.html

[49] Know to be useful or believe to be beautiful
William Morris "The Beauty of Life," a lecture before the Birmingham Society of Arts and School of Design (19 February 1880), later published in *Hopes and Fears for Art: Five Lectures Delivered in Birmingham, London, and Nottingham, 1878-1881* (1882).
http://en.wikiquote.org/wiki/William_Morris

[50] Stephanie Winston on Getting Organized
Getting Organized: The Easy Way to Put Your Life in Order by Stephanie Winston, Updated and Revised, Warner, 1991. The crucial three questions are on page 179.

[51] Paperless
David Sparks is the author of *Paperless*, iBooks, 2012. You can download the book—and lots of other wonderfully useful information for simplifying your electronic life—at http://macsparky.com/paperless/

[52] Patriotism is, fundamentally, a conviction
George Bernard Shaw, in *The World* (15 November 1893). Cited in *Not Bloody Likely! And Other Quotations from Bernard Shaw*, Columbia University Press, 1996, page 142.
http://en.wikiquote.org/wiki/Patriotism

[53] **A wee book that suggested ways to apply the ancient Rule**
John McQuiston II, *Always We Begin Again: The Benedictine Way of Living*, Morehouse, 1996.

[54] **I could do my own version of Columbo**
Peter Falk, who played Columbo, wrote a memoir entitled *Just One More Thing* Hutchinson, 2007. Mark Dawidziak has compiled the *Columbo Phile: A Casebook*, Time Warner, 1989, as a summary of the TV series. The complete set of *Columbo* films is available on 35 DVDs from Universal—in a cigar box! Just one more thing: this complete set contains all 69 episodes in which Peter Falk appeared as Columbo. He solves all 69 cases—including the very first one (called *Prescription: Murder*) in which Columbo says for the first time: "There's just one more thing, sir."

Chapter 2: The Shucket List

[55] **To attain knowledge**
http://self-realisation.com/auto-didactic/the-wisdom-of-lao-tzu/ For a wonderfully witty and enlightening introduction to the ideas of Lao Tzu—as well as some excellent suggestions on how to Shucket—we recommend *Trying Not To Try: The Art of Effortlessness and the Power of Spontaneity* by Edward Slingerland, Canongate, 2014.

[56] **Grook—a playful kind of poetry invented by Piet Hein**
Piet Hein, *Grooks*, Doubleday, 1966. Since Piet Hein's books are now out of print, you can find some of the grooks online, for instance at http://www.poemhunter.com/piet-hein/ Walt's well-worn and well-loved copy of *Grooks* contains dozens of gems. Here is an example, called *The Eternal Twins:*
Taking fun
as simply fun
and earnestness
in earnest
shows how thoroughly
thou none
of the two
discernest.

57 Take off all your envies
This quotation is attributed to Cesare Pavese, but without a specific source.
http://www.brainyquote.com/quotes/authors/c/cesare_pavese.html
Pavese's words are cited by Marshall Rosenberg in his NVC workshops, as seen at http://www.youtube.com/watch?v=Ql5hywRyqgo

58 A thousand memories and not a single regret
These are the last lines of *Fiddler Jones* from *Spoon River Anthology,* by Edgar Lee Masters. The poem was first published in 1915. Our source is pages 27 and 28 of the Dover edition of 1992. It is also in *The Oxford Book of American Verse*, edited by F. O. Matthiessen, Oxford, 1950. The poem begins with these lines:

> *The earth keeps some vibration going*
> *There in your heart, and that is you.*
> *And if the people find you can fiddle,*
> *Why, fiddle you must, for all your life.*

And then ends with these lines:

> *I ended up with a broken fiddle—*
> *And a broken laugh, and a thousand memories,*
> *And not a single regret.*

59 Non, Je ne regrette rien
Edith Piaf became known to newer generations through the film *La Vie en Rose*. She had already made this song famous. The music and lyrics of *Non, Je Ne Regrette Rien* are by Charles Dumont and Michel Vaucaire.
http://www.metrolyrics.com/non-je-ne-regrette-rien-lyrics-edith-piaf.html#ixzz2rVgj3QsV

60 Statute of limitations on childhood traumas
Gordon Livingstone in *Too Soon Old; Too Late Smart: 20 Things You Need to Know Now!* Marlowe, 2004.

61 If you are irritated by every rub
https://www.goodreads.com/author/quotes/875661.Rumi

[62] Marquis of Montrose

For more information on James Graham, the first Marquis of Montrose, see
http://en.wikipedia.org/wiki/James_Graham,_1st_Marquess_of_Montros
e or go to http://www.montrose-society.org.uk/index.htm where you can
find an extensive bibliography and you can listen to Steeleye Span sing
"Montrose" to give you a short but musical experience of his life and his
poetry.

And if you really want to know about *The Last Campaign of Montrose*,
then you could go to the Library of the University of Edinburgh and see
if they still have a copy of the M.Litt. thesis that I submitted more than
40 years ago.

[63] This play of old sorrow, written in tears and blood

Walt's well-marked copy is *Long Day's Journey into Night*, Jonathan
Cape, 1966. On the dedication page, Eugene O'Neill puts this message:

*For Carlotta, on our 12th Wedding Anniversary. Dearest: I give you the
original script of this play of old sorrow, written in tears and blood. A
sadly inappropriate gift, it would seem, for a day celebrating happiness.
But you will understand. I mean it as a tribute to your love and
tenderness which gave me the faith in love that enabled me to face my
dead at last and write this play—write it with deep pity and
understanding and forgiveness for all the four haunted Tyrones. These
twelve years, Beloved One, have been a Journey into Light—into love.*

You know my gratitude. And my love!

Gene

Tao House, July 22, 1941

[64] I'm interested in the future

Charles Franklin Kettering (1876-1958) was an inventor, engineer,
businessman, and the holder of 186 patents. He was another Ohio boy!
We cannot find the direct source of this quotation, although it is on the
web in various versions. You can read more about him at
http://en.wikipedia.org/wiki/Charles_F._Kettering

⁶⁵ **The difference between [human] and [alien]**
Orson Scott Card, *Speaker for the Dead*, Tor, 1986, page 1.

⁶⁶ **Seven learnings about diversity**
For more on the seven learnings about diversity and the seven isms, see the Learnings section of Walt's website at
http://www.walthopkins.com/en/writings/learnings/seven-learnings-about-diversity,40.html

⁶⁷ **And did you get what you wanted from this life, even so?**
Raymond Carver (1938-1988) wrote poems and short stories. *Late Fragment* is the last poem in *A New Path to the Waterfall*, Grove Press, 1989, written when Carver was dying of cancer.

⁶⁸ **When I'm facilitating a T Group**
T stands for Training. A T Group is an intensive experience in which a small group of people sit together in a circle. Although there is a trainer or facilitator, that person does not lead the group and is often silent. There is no fixed agenda. So people talk—or are silent—and gradually learn about themselves, each other, and groups.

For more about the history, experiences, and possibilities of T Groups, see the *Reading Book for Human Relations*, 8th Edition (NTL Institute for Applied Behavioral Science, 1999). You could begin with the chapters on the *History of NTL: A Story Worth Sharing* by Warren B. Clayton and Donna G. Lucas and *The Power of Imagining Positively: T Group Possibilities* by Jane Magruder Watkins, Cathy Royal, and Walt Hopkins.

To participate in a T Group, contact Walt or the NTL Institute at
www.ntl.org

⁶⁹ **Herb Shepard, one of the creators of Organization Development**
Herb inspired and trained a generation of OD consultants. You can learn more about him through the Herbert Shepard Foundation at
www.HerbertShepard.org Among Herb's many publications, two are particularly worth reading. Fortunately, those two are both available online, although in edited versions.

The first is about life planning and begins with the memorable sentence: "Life planning is planning life-worth-living." See this essay at http://www.executive.org/shepard/2014-06-26-Herbert-Shepard_Charting-the-Life-of-Your-Choice.pdf The second essay is often referred to as Rules of Thumb for Change Agents and is at http://www.executive.org/shepard/2014-06-26-Herbert-Shepard_Moving-Forward-in-Your-Organization-and_Community.pdf

[70] **Art is the elimination of the unnecessary**
http://www.pablopicasso.org/Quotes.jsp

[71] **Removing all the marble that was not part of the statue**
Giorgio Vasari (1511-1574), a contemporary of Michelangelo, was an Italian painter, architect, historian, and author of *Lives of the Most Excellent Painters, Sculptors, and Architects*. You can read Vasari's work online, for instance at http://employees.oneonta.edu/farberas/arth/Arth213/michelangelo_vasari.html

[72] **Less is more**
This quotation first appears in the 1855 poem *Andrea del Sarto, (Called "The Faultless Painter")* by the English poet Robert Browning (1812-1889). Andrea del Sarto was another Michelangelo contemporary. Read the poem at http://www.poetryfoundation.org/poem/173001

[73] **And if you are still learning to use those chisels like Michelangelo**
Walt's note: After many years of quoting Vasari on Michelangelo's approach to sculpture, I was delighted to read in Edward Slingerland's book on Chinese philosophy that not only is there an ancient Chinese story about an artist named Qing who approaches art in the same way as Michelangelo, but there is actually a direct quotation on this idea from Michelangelo himself.

On page 231 of *Trying Not to Try: The Art of Effortlessness and the Power of Spontaneity*, Canongate, 2014, Slingerland quotes a sonnet attributed to Michelangelo.

The source is Michelangelo Buonarroti, *Rime e prose di Michelagnolo Buonarroti, pittore, scultore, architetto, e poeta fiorentino*, Milan, G. Silvestri.

Non ha l'ottimo artista alcun concetto
Ch'un marmo solo in se non circoscriva
Col suo soverchio, e solo a quello arriva
La man che obbedisce all'intelleto

Slingerland gives thanks to Giovanna Lammers for help with his translation:

"No artist, no matter how excellent, possesses an idea that is not already contained in the marble block, imprisoned by superfluous matter that only the hand guided by the intellect can remove."

Chapter 3: The Ducket List

[74] **Look on every exit being an entrance somewhere else**
This is from Tom Stoppard, *Rosencrantz and Guildenstern are Dead,* Faber and Faber, 1967, page 20. Tom Stoppard is a Czech-born British playwright, screenwriter, and author. This line is part of a speech by the Player: *We keep to our usual stuff, more or less, only inside out. We do on stage the things that are supposed to happen off. Which is a kind of integrity, if you look on every exit being an entrance somewhere else.*

[75] **SIETAR**
The Society for Intercultural Education Training and Research (SIETAR) is a professional organization for those working with intercultural issues in Organizations, Education, Social and Political domains as well as the Media and the Arts. http://www.sietareu.org/

[76] **Connection Scan**
This tool is found at http://connection-scan.com

[77] **David Steindl-Rast**
Brother David Steindl-Rast is a Catholic Benedictine monk of Mount Savior Monastery in New York. He might best be described as an

"apostle of gratefulness" who encourages a balance between active and contemplative life. He worked with George to create an experimental monastery for Oberlin College students during a winter term in the 1970's.

[78] When they tell me I'm too old to do something, I attempt it immediately

Here are Picasso's words in the original: *Cuando me dicen que soy demasiado viejo para hacer una cosa, procuro hacerla enseguida.*
http://es.wikiquote.org/wiki/Pablo_Picasso

[79] How hard it is to keep from being king

The poem *How Hard It Is to Keep from Being King When It's in You and in the Situation* starts on page 74 in Robert Frost, *In the Clearing*, Holt, Rinehart and Winston, 1962. Further along in the poem, on page 81, there is another good Ducket line: "The only certain freedom's in departure."

[80] Paperless

David Sparks is the author of *Paperless*, iBooks, 2012, as well as a book on managing your email. You can download both at
http://macsparky.com/

[81] OmniFocus task manager software

You can download this software at
https://www.omnigroup.com/omnifocus#

[82] OmniFocus process is helpfully explained by David Sparks

You can download the *OmniFocus Video Field Guide* by David Sparks at http://macsparky.com/omnifocus/

[83] A thousand memories and not a single thing to dust

This is a riff on "a thousand memories and not a single regret" from *Fiddler Jones* in the *Spoon River Anthology* by Edgar Lee Masters. Our source is page 28 of the Dover edition of 1992.

[84] The world is too much with us

William Wordsworth (1770-1850) was a leading Romantic poet. *The World Is Too Much With Us; Late and Soon* was first published in *Poems, In Two Volumes* (1807). Our source is page 626 of *The New Oxford Book of English Verse*, chosen and edited by Sir Arthur Quiller-Couch, Oxford, 1955.

Chapter 4: The Fucket List

[85] Profanity provides a relief denied even to prayer
Our source is Albert Bigelow Paine, *Mark Twain, A Biography: The Personal and Literary Life of Samuel Langhorne Clemens*, Harper, 1912, Chapter 38.

Thanks to the amazing Project Gutenberg that provides access to the full text of out-of-copyright books at www.gutenberg.org, we found the source of this quotation at http://www.gutenberg.org/files/2988/2988-h/2988-h.htm In appreciation, we have made a donation to Project Gutenberg.

[86] Habits allow us to not think about what we're doing
Alex Levin, *Teacher Training*. She is Director of the In-Depth Teacher Training Programs at Sun and Moon Yoga Studio in Arlington, Virginia. http://www.sunandmoonstudio.com/Features/levin.shtml

[87] Started each day by playing Bach on his piano
http://www.concierto.org/artists/item/826-con-pablo-casals-eng

[88] The weird and wonderful Urban Dictionary website
http://www.urbandictionary.com

[89] Dick Bolles wrote a wonderful book called *The Three Boxes of Life*
Richard N. Bolles, *The Three Boxes of Life: And How To Get Out of Them*, Ten Speed Press, 1976.

[90] Charlie Seashore's great wisdom
For more about the wisdom and work of both Charles and Edith Seashore, see: http://www.strategy-business.com/article/06499?pg=all

⁹¹ **Even if diversity is not on the agenda**
For more of Walt's learnings about diversity, see *I'm a Straight White Guy—So What's Diversity Got To Do With Me?* in *Reading Book for Human Relations Training,* 8th Edition, NTL Institute for Applied Behavioral Science, 1991, pages 121-125. You can also find a summary at http://www.walthopkins.com/en/writings/learnings/seven-learnings-about-diversity,40.html

⁹² **The courage to change the things that should be changed**
This prayer is often adapted to sound something like this: *God, grant us the serenity to accept the things we cannot change, the courage to change the things we can, and the wisdom to know the difference.*

We much prefer Reinhold Niebuhr's own version: *God, give me grace to accept with serenity the things that cannot be changed, Courage to change the things which should be changed, and the Wisdom to distinguish the one from the other.* See http://en.wikipedia.org/wiki/Serenity_Prayer

⁹³ **How long are you going to stay angry?**
Bertolt Brecht, *Mother Courage,* translated by Eric Bentley, Doubleday, 1955.

⁹⁴ **Keep feedback and Change feedback**
For more of Walt's learnings on feedback, see http://www.walthopkins.com/en/writings/learnings/feedback-keep-and-change,48.html

⁹⁵ **The dangers of trying to cure other people**
David Keirsey and Marilyn Bates, *Please Understand Me,* Prometheus Nemesis, 1984.

⁹⁶ **Dan Saffer coined the term topless meetings**
For more information about Dan Saffer, go to http://about.me/dansaffer

⁹⁷ **Seven Learnings on Retreat**
See http://www.walthopkins.com/en/writings/learnings/seven-learnings-on-retreat,37.html

[98] **Here Be Dragons—and Dreams**
For the rest of this issue of Learnings, see *Here Be Dragons—and Dreams* at http://www.walthopkins.com/en/writings/learnings/here-be-dragons---and-dreams,45.html

[99] **I am speaking of the kind of risk-taking**
James Lipton, *Here Be Dragons*, published as the *My Turn* column in the *Newsweek* issue of December 6, 1976. Walt has the original page from *Newsweek*, carefully preserved in a binder of things *Worth Remembering*.

[100] **The psychological term is introjection**
For an explanation of introjection, see Frederick Perls, Ralph F. Hefferline, and Paul Goodman, *Gestalt Therapy: Excitement and Growth in the Human Personality*, Dell, 1951. The chapter on Introjection begins on page 189. The Gestalt approach includes a focus on the here and now, a cycle of experience from awareness to excitement to contact to withdrawal, and a sense of personal responsibility.

[101] **What do you care what other people think?**
Do read some of the wonderful stories in Richard P. Feynman, *What Do You Care What Other People Think?* Harper Collins, 1989.

[102] **There is some necessity for being, or learning to be...independent**
Letter to Walt Hopkins from W. Dean Hopkins on 5 November 1964.

[103] **I do my thing, and you do your thing**
Frederick S. Perls, *Gestalt Therapy Verbatim*, Real People Press, 1969. The Gestalt Prayer is on page 4.

Chapter 5: The Plucket List

[104] **One great thing about growing old**
Joseph Campbell, *A Joseph Campbell Companion: Reflections on the Art of Living,* Harper Perennial, 1995.

[105] **I've waited all my life/If not now, when will I?**
http://www.last.fm/music/Incubus/_/If+Not+Now,+When%3F

[106] **Here's something to remember when you're older**
This is a line from *The Bucket List,* 2007, written by Justin Zackham and directed by Rob Reiner. See the whole list of quotations at
http://www.imdb.com/title/tt0825232/trivia?tab=qt&ref_=tt_trv_qu

[107] **The wise man pees when he can**
Despite various web searches, we cannot find a confirmation that Wellington actually said this. Let us know if you have a source!

[108] **God made man because He loves stories**
Elie Wiesel, *The Gates of the Forest: A Novel*, Schocken Books, 1995.

[109] **The tree laden with fruit always bends low**
http://www.rkmathnagpur.org/sri_ramakrishna/teachings_sr.htm

[110] **Remember when the music**
Harry Chapin's lyrics are at
http://www.metrolyrics.com/remember-when-the-music-lyrics-harry-chapin.html But do download the song and listen to him sing it!

[111] **Take hold of something and quickly remove it from its place**
This definition comes from the online version of the Oxford Dictionaries at http://www.oxforddictionaries.com/definition/english/pluck
The usages by Shakespeare and others are in the *Oxford English Dictionary*, Oxford University Press, 1933.

[112] **I'm the kind who likes to grasp his dream like flesh**
Line 877 in Book Two of *The Odyssey: A Modern Sequel* by Nikos Kazantzakis, translated by Kimon Friar, Simon and Schuster, 1958.

[113] **Beyond The Fuck It**
The story of BTFI is on page 120 of *The Art of Possibility: Transforming Professional and Personal Life* by Rosamund Stone Zander and Benjamin Zander, Harvard Business School Press, 2000.

[114] **There are flowers everywhere—for those who bother to look**
http://www.quotery.com/quotes/there-are-flowers-everywhere-for-those-who-bother-to-look/
Henri Matisse definitely bothered to look!

[115] **How did it get so late so soon?**
Dr. Seuss wrote:
"How did it get so late so soon?
It's night before it's afternoon.
December is here before it's June.
My goodness how the time has flewn.
How did it get so late so soon?"
http://izquotes.com/author/dr.-seuss

[116] **I skate to where the puck is going to be**
http://www.brainyquote.com/quotes/quotes/w/waynegretz383282.html

[117] **You miss 100% of the shots you don't take**
https://www.goodreads.com/author/quotes/240132.Wayne_Gretzky

[118] **You see things; and you say "Why?"**
George Bernard Shaw's play *Back to Methuselah* from 1921 is the original source, although many of us first learned this wisdom from Bobby Kennedy's paraphrase: "Some people see things as they are and say why? I dream things that never were and say, why not?"
http://www.quotecounterquote.com/2011/07/i-dream-things-that-never-were-and-say.html

[119] **Wise folk learn when they can, fools learn when they must**
Personal communication from Peter Honey on 4 June 2014: *"Yes, I think Wellington was reputed to have said, 'Wise men pee when they can, fools pee when they must' but I could never verify it either. Anyway, I immediately adapted it to, 'Wise folk learn when they can, fools learn when they must'. As you realise, it is rather a neat way of promoting the idea of voluntary learning as opposed to compulsory learning. I'd be delighted to be quoted."* Peter Honey and Alan Mumford are the creators of the *Honey and Mumford Learning Styles Questionnaire*, available at
http://www.peterhoney.com/content/tools-learningstyles.html

¹²⁰ **I always remember you like the long shot**
Personal communication from Giles Hopkins on 5 November 2012.

¹²¹ **Reach what you cannot**
Nikos Kazantzakis, *Report to Greco*, translated by P.A. Bien, Bantam, 1966, page 17.

¹²² **Keep on keeping on**
For more of Roy's wisdom and some suggestions for avoiding re-TIRE-ment with a Do-It-Yourself Re-FIRE-ment Kit, see Roy P. Fairfield, *Get Inspired! Releasing Your Creative Self at Any Age,* Prometheus Books, 2001. Here are some of the chapter titles in that book: *Crap Detecting as a Way of Life, Self-Fulfilling and Self-Deceiving Prophecies, Learning as a Subversive Activity,* and *Spontaneity and Being.* Enjoy!

¹²³ **He either fears his fate too much**
This version of Montrose's poem is from page 465 in Volume Two of *Memorials of Montrose and His Times*, edited by Mark Napier, Maitland Club, 1850. Forty years ago I borrowed this book from the University of Edinburgh's library, kept it on my desk for months, and eventually took it back. Now I can go online through the Internet Archive and find the same book digitized by the National Library of Scotland at
https://archive.org/details/memorialsofmontr02mait

¹²⁴ **True stories of people who influenced pluckily**
The first three stories are taken from page 166 of *Influencing for Results in Organisations* by Walt Hopkins, Libri Publishing, 2012.

¹²⁵ **In my work I have discovered Flow**
Flow: The Psychology of Optimal Experience by Mihaly Csikszentmihalyi, Harper Perennial, 2008.

¹²⁶ **In his brilliant expositions of love**
See and hear Yann Dall'Aglio at
http://www.youtube.com/watch?v=dJgiYBdD2VA

¹²⁷ **Life is either a daring adventure, or nothing**
Helen Keller, *Let Us Have Faith*, Doubleday, 1940.

[128] The truth is that there is only one terminal dignity—love
http://en.wikiquote.org/wiki/Helen_Hayes

Chapter 6: The Trucket List

[129] **If I should not be learning now, when should I be?**
Apparently, this is the response from Lacydes when someone asked him
why he was studying geometry late in his life.
https://thedailyextract.wordpress.com/2014/09/07/if-i-should-not-be-learning-now-when-should-i-ge-lacydes/ Lacydes of Cyrene was a
Greek philosopher who headed the Academy at Athens for 26 years
from 241 BC.
http://en.wikipedia.org/wiki/Lacydes_of_Cyrene

[130] **Keep on Truckin'**
Keep on Truckin' (as in "keep on moving") is a phrase that became
famous from a cartoon drawn by Robert Crumb, first published in *Zap
Comix* in 1968. The phrase apparently originated in a blues song sung by
Blind Boy Fuller in the 1930s. Crumb's drawings became iconic images
of optimism during the hippie era.
http://en.wikipedia.org/wiki/Keep_on_Truckin'_

[131] **It ain't over 'til it's over**
The lyrics by Lenny Kravitz, from his 1991 album *Mama Said*, are at
http://www.azlyrics.com/lyrics/lennykravitz/itaintovertilitsover.html

[132] **It ain't over 'til it's over**
The story of Yogi's great line in 1973 is on page 121 of *The Yogi Book*
by Yogi Berra, Workman Publishing, 1998.

[133] **Coming in on whichever beat felt right at the moment**
Yes to the Mess: Surprising Leadership Lessons from Jazz by Frank
Barrett, Harvard Business Review Press, 2012.

[134] **If a man does not keep pace with his companions**
Henry David Thoreau, *Walden*, first published in 1854. This line comes
in Chapter 18. If you don't already have this, we can now recommend an
annotated version online: http://thoreau.eserver.org/walden18.html

[135] **Use of Self as Instrument**
For examples in Individual Development, see the section on *Therapist Is His Own Instrument*, beginning on page 18 of *Gestalt Therapy Integrated: Contours of Theory and Practice* by Erving and Miriam Polster, Brunner/Mazel, 1973.

For examples in Organization Development, see *Organization Development Classics: The Practice and Theory of Change—The Best of the OD Practitioner*, edited by Donald F. Van Eynde, Judith C. Hoy, and Dixie Cody Van Eynde, Jossey-Bass, 1997. Part Three of this book has brilliant essays by Herb Shepard, Bob Tannenbaum, David Noer, Saul Eisen, George T. Lynn, Tom Isgar, Geoffrey Bellman, Natasha Josfeowitz, and Dave Jamieson.

[136] **Old-timer. Driven for over 70 years**
In German, the tee shirt reads: *Oldtimer über 70 Jahre gelaufen, kein Rost, nur leichte Gebrauchsspuren, Topzustand.*

[137] **A Third Act**
See *Life's Third Act*, this inspiring TED Talk by Jane Fonda, at
http://www.ted.com/talks/jane_fonda_life_s_third_act.html

[138] **Cultural Competence**
For information on the game that George has created on this, see
http://diversophy.com/collections/global/products/cultural-competence

[139] **Farid Elashmawi was both a colleague and friend**
Author of *Competing Globally,* Routledge, 2001.

[140] **Runa Mackay...wrote a book on Palestine**
Runa Mackay, *Exile in Israel: A Personal Journey with the Palestinians,* Wild Goose Publications, 1995.

[141] **What I wrote about my mother for her 80th birthday**
For the whole essay on my mother for her 80th birthday, see
http://www.walthopkins.com/en/writings/learnings/a-goodly-heritage,53.html

¹⁴² **I made a difference for that one**
Loren Eiseley, *The Star Thrower*, Mariner, 1979. For more information, see: http://en.wikipedia.org/wiki/The_Star_Thrower

¹⁴³ **The book that I wrote on influencing skills**
Walt Hopkins, *Influencing for Results in Organisations*, Libri Publishing, 2012, is available at http://www.libripublishing.co.uk/management-policy-and-education/influencing-for-results-in-organisations

¹⁴⁴ **Seven learnings about journaling**
Journaling in Small Groups by Walt Hopkins, NTL Institute, 2006. George's book on journaling is *Keeping Your Personal Journal*, Ballantine Books, 1978. We aim to have both of them available online—so contact us via https://www.facebook.com/bucketbookviews

¹⁴⁵ **The Fairfield-Hopkins Time-Stretch Phenomenon**
For more about the Fairfield-Hopkins Time-Stretch Phenomenon, see *Journaling in Small Groups* by Walt Hopkins, NTL Institute, 2006.

¹⁴⁶ **Seven things I learned from Roy**
See the Learnings at www.WaltHopkins.com

¹⁴⁷ **SIETAR Europa**
SIETAR is a professional organization for those engaged in intercultural work of all kinds. See http://www.sietareu.org/

¹⁴⁸ **Real communication is cohabitation**
Informer n'est pas communiquer (Sending information is not communication) http://www.wolton.cnrs.fr/spip.php?article20

Chapter 7: The Tucket List

¹⁴⁹ **I celebrate myself, and sing myself**
Walt Whitman, *Song of Myself*, originally published in 1855. Our source is page 279 of *The Oxford Book of American Verse*, edited by F. O. Matthiessen, Oxford University Press, 1950.

[150] **A tucket is a fanfare—a trumpet blast with a roll of drums**
Although we still search online for definitions and other things, we also
return regularly to the books on our shelves, and we have done so for
tuck and tucket. In Walt's case, that means pulling down *The Compact
Edition of the Oxford English Dictionary*, Oxford University Press,
1971, which reduces the original 1933 ten-volume edition to two
volumes by printing four original pages on each new page—and
including a magnifying glass with the set!

[151] **Low self-esteem is like driving through life with your handbrake**
Maxwell Maltz wrote several books on his theories of positive thinking,
including *Psycho-Cybernetics*, Wilshire, 1969.

[152] **Marshall Rosenberg suggests that the emptiness**
There is a full video presentation of Marshall Rosenberg's training at
https://www.youtube.com/watch?v=Ql5hywRyqgo

[153] **I was born modest. But it wore off.**
Note from Walt: Although I have not found a written source for this, I
have something better to offer. I have the original record from 1959 of
Hal Holbrook appearing as Mark Twain in *Mark Twain Tonight!* on
Broadway. I remember going to that show with my family and then
memorizing the lines as I listened to the recording over and over again.
So I trust Hal Holbrook, who has done massive research on Twain, to
have found the line somewhere. The recording is now available on
iTunes and a DVD is at
http://www.kulturvideo.com/SearchResults.asp?Search=hal+holbrook

[154] **If a man does not keep pace with his companions**
Henry David Thoreau, *Walden*, first published in 1854. This line comes
in Chapter 18. An annotated version online is the source we now
recommend: http://thoreau.eserver.org/walden18.html

[155] **Our task here is to inspire and to be inspired**
You can learn more about Dr. Dina Glouberman's writings and
Imagework approach at http://www.dinaglouberman.com. Or pick up
one of her books, such as *The Joy of Burnout: How the end of the world
can be a new beginning* by Dina Glouberman, Skyros, 2002.

[156] What kind of world do you want?

To download Jim Lord's book, go to
http://www.jimlord.org/world/what-kind-of-world-do-you-want

[157] Write a series of stories about good times in his life

The work I describe here is my own version of what I began learning from John Crystal and Dick Bolles back in 1976. See John C. Crystal and Richard N. Bolles, *Where Do I Go From Here With My Life?* Ten Speed Press, 1974; Richard N. Bolles, *The Three Boxes of Life: And How To Get Out of Them*, Ten Speed Press, 1976; and the latest edition (he revises it annually) of Richard N. Bolles, *What Color Is Your Parachute?* Ten Speed Press. Dick Bolles is still going strong in his late 80s. See his latest ideas on living and on job-hunting at
http://www.jobhuntersbible.com

[158] This is what I call a Serious Dream

A Goal Is A Dream Taken Seriously: The Castle Approach to Career & Life Design by Walt Hopkins. This is a poster with a guidebook that was published in 1986 by Organisation Design & Development. They no longer offer it, but I still get requests for it, so it is on my Trucket List to issue a new version—after we finish this book!

[159] Some current research

For brief report on this, see, "The Powerlessness of Positive Thinking" by Adam Alter
http://www.newyorker.com/online/blogs/currency/2014/02/the-powerlessness-of-positive-thinking.html

[160] Measure yourself by the people who measure themselves by you

Justin Zackham, the screenwriter, talks about this line in an interview:

Oh, absolutely. The thing I want to say also about the movie is that it ultimately is not about the list. The one thing that those two guys don't have on the list, which is the one thing they really get, is a best friend. They don't put it down, but yet at the end they've got someone who loves them, who they've been through this experience with. They've taught each other. They've grown from it. And the thing for me is the line that really started the script for me. Morgan says in the opening voiceover that you measure yourself by the people who measure themselves by you. I wrote that about my group of friends. And sort of just like Rob said, are you doing the best with the people who love you and who you love in the world. Everything else on the list, that's driving yourself, but to me that's what the movie's about. We talked about that over and over and that's really what the spirit of it is.

You can find the complete interview at:
http://cinema.com/articles/5504/bucket-list-the-rob-reiner-and-justin-zackham-q-and.phtml

[161] **Only when the sense of the pain of others begins does man begin**
The Collected Poems, 1952-1990: Yevgeny Yevtushenko, Henry Holt & Co.,1992.

Epilogue: Beyond the ...ucket Lists

[162] **A goal is a dream taken seriously**
A Goal Is A Dream Taken Seriously: The Castle Approach to Career & Life Design by Walt Hopkins. This is a poster with a guidebook that was published in 1986 by Organisation Design & Development. They no longer offer it, but (as I've said already a few endnotes before this one) I still get requests for it, so it is on my Trucket List to issue a new version—after we finish this book!

[163] **Do everything with thanksgiving**
Philippians 4:6, *The Bible.*

[164] **Give, and it will be given to you**
Luke 6:38, *The Bible.*

[165] **Surprised by joy—impatient as the wind**
The first words of a poem by the 19th century English poet, William Wordsworth. This theme was picked up by C. S. Lewis, another English writer, a century later, as the title of his autobiography. While Wordsworth's poem was a lament for his untimely deceased daughter, Lewis's autobiography is about man's search for happiness in the fickle fortunes of life.

[166] **The world is a world of tears**
Book I, line 462 of the *Aeneid* by the Roman poet Virgil.

[167] **Have you anything to declare?**
The book has been reprinted as late as 2010 and is available at:
http://www.faber.co.uk/catalog/have-you-anything-to-declare/9780571273058

[168] **We look forward to seeing you online**
Please clog our blog at https://www.facebook.com/bucketbookviews
We look forward to meeting you and hearing and sharing what we have in common and the surprises we can bring to each other.

[169] **I wonder if they miss me, as long as I make history**
http://www.azlyrics.com/lyrics/asaprocky/longliveaap.html

[170] **As a low lantern's flame flicks in its final blaze**
These are lines 1305 to 1308 in Book 23 of *The Odyssey: A Modern Sequel,* an epic poem by Greek poet and philosopher Nikos Kazantzakis, translated by Kimon Friar, Simon & Schuster, 1958.

Thanks for reading our book.

We look forward to talking with you online at
https://www.facebook.com/bucketbookviews